"Through his wise writings, Jerry Bridges has become a pastor to my soul. Here, with his usual profound simplicity, he gives biblically balanced perspective on the hard questions of human suffering and the sovereignty of God. *Is God Really in Control?* will comfort those who mourn and help hurting people understand the ways of God."

— PHILIP GRAHAM RYKEN, senior minister,
Tenth Presbyterian Church, Philadelphia

"Sanity, realism, authenticity, and personal integrity are the hallmarks of all Jerry Bridges' writing. Now he brings these qualities to bear upon the hard question of suffering. Cheap, easy, and—ultimately—cruel answers are ten a penny today. In sharp contrast, *Is God Really in Control?* addresses the issues in a healthy, biblical way. Its message will help bring much-needed spiritual stability and comfort."

— SINCLAIR B. FERGUSON, author of *Deserted By God?*

IS GOD REALLY
IN CONTROL?

TRUSTING GOD IN A WORLD OF HURT

JERRY BRIDGES

NAVPRESS®

A NavPress resource published in alliance
with Tyndale House Publishers, Inc.

NavPress is the publishing ministry of The Navigators, an international Christian organization and leader in personal spiritual development. NavPress is committed to helping people grow spiritually and enjoy lives of meaning and hope through personal and group resources that are biblically rooted, culturally relevant, and highly practical.

For more information, visit www.NavPress.com.

For information about special discounts for bulk purchases, please contact Tyndale House Publishers at csresponse@tyndale.com, or call 1-800-323-9400.

Library of Congress Cataloging-in-Publication Data

Bridges, Jerry.
   Is God really in control? : trusting God in a world of hurt / Jerry Bridges
      p. cm.
   Includes bibliographical references (p.149-154).
   ISBN 1-57683-931-1
1. Suffering—Religious aspects—Christianity. 2. Trust in God—Christianity. I. Title.
   BV4909.B74 2006
   248.8'6—dc22

ISBN 978-1-57683-931-7

2005028182

Printed in the United States of America

23 22 21 20
15 14 13 12 11

To
Tom and Sue Lutz and the congregation of
Edgewood Baptist Church

CONTENTS

PREFACE

On Monday morning, August 29, 2005, a large section of the 17th Street canal levee in New Orleans gave way to the storm surge caused by Hurricane Katrina. Within a few hours, two more levees would burst, flooding 80 percent of the city. Though the toll of the disaster is still being counted as I write these words, the devastation is already considered the worst natural disaster to hit the United States since the San Francisco earthquake of 1906, which killed 6,000 people.

Etched in our memories is also the day after Christmas 2004, when an earthquake 700 miles long beneath the Indian Ocean created a tsunami that caused the deaths of more than 200,000 people and displaced millions more in Southeast Asia.

Yet other kinds of tragedies haunt our time. On July 7, 2005, four powerful explosions rocked London's transportation system, killing more than 50 people and injuring at least 700. It was the worst terrorist attack in Britain since World War II. A similar incident, though even more deadly, occurred in Madrid in March 2004. And even more devastating to human lives and property than these were the horrific 9/11 terrorist attacks on New York City and Washington, DC.

The question on many people's lips is: Where is God in all of this? And perhaps even more urgently: Where is He concerning the adversities in my personal life? In the midst of such questioning, it has seemed to me time to reexamine a message I wrote in the late 1980s—at a time prior to many of the tragedies mentioned above—and ask this question again of the Scriptures: Is God really in control?

My earlier book *Trusting God* was the fruit of a lengthy Bible study on the subject of God's sovereignty in the affairs of His people. During the four years of my study, I encountered many other people who were struggling with some of the same issues I was: Does God actually control the circumstances of our lives, or do "bad" things just happen to us because we live in a sin-cursed world? If God really does control the circumstances of our lives, why did He allow my friend to get cancer? Can I truly trust God when the going gets tough in different areas of my life?

In the years since *Trusting God* was published, much has changed in the complexion of our world. Yet I am convinced that the message God would have us hear today has not changed. This new book, then, summarizes my ongoing wrestling with this very difficult—but finally comforting—theological issue. It was born out of the results of addressing needs in my own life and realizing that many other believers have similar questions and doubts. It is written from the perspective of a brother and companion to all those who are tempted at times to ask, "Can I really trust God?"

As I have spoken on this topic over the last fifteen years, I have become much more aware of the widespread and frequent occurrences of adversity around me. I had not realized as acutely as I do now the pervasive nature of suffering and heartache, especially among those who follow Christ. As a result of my heightened perception of suffering around me, I found myself frequently asking, "Do I truly believe what I am writing?"

Another difficulty for me has been the realization that many of my friends have experienced far greater adversity than I have. Who am I to seek to write words of instruction and encouragement to them, when I have not experienced the measure of pain they have? My answer to that question is the realization that the truth of God's

Word and the encouragement it is intended to give is not dependent upon my experience. I have not written this book about my experiences, which are not particularly unusual. I have written it as a Bible study about God and His sovereignty, wisdom, and love as they bear upon the adversities we all encounter.

Is God Really in Control? is written for the average person who has not necessarily experienced major catastrophe but who does frequently encounter the typical adversities and heartaches of life: the pregnancy miscarriage, the lost job, the auto accident, the rebellious son or daughter, the unfair professor in college. These events do not make "front page" news; indeed, they are often buried within a broken or confused heart.

I sincerely hope that none of the statements I make in the following chapters come across as glib and easy answers to the difficult problems of adversity and suffering. There are no easy answers. Adversity is difficult even when we know God is in control of our circumstances. In fact, that knowledge sometimes tends to aggravate the pain. "If God is in control," we ask, "why did He allow this to happen?"

Most of the content of this new book appeared in my earlier *Trusting God*. My purpose in creating this new book is twofold: First, I desire for a new generation of readers to glorify God by acknowledging His sovereignty and goodness. Second, I desire to encourage God's people in a post-9/11 world by demonstrating from Scripture that God is in control of their lives, that He does indeed love them, and that He works out all the circumstances of their lives for their ultimate good.

The reader will notice an abundance of quotations from other writers. This book, though, is not merely a synthesis of other people's views. The basic convictions stated in these chapters are the result of my own personal Bible study done over a long period of time. I acknowledge, however, my indebtedness to other writers for affirmation and, in some instances, clarification of my understanding of some of these truths.

You will find that I often go back to the English Puritans (and their more recent theological heirs) as well as the Dutch theologian G. C. Berkouwer. The Puritans of the sixteenth and seventeenth centuries wrestled hard with the issue of God's sovereignty, partly because of persecution for their faith. I believe their voices (as well as those writing in their tradition) can continue to instruct us in our uncertain time. Professor Berkouwer, on the other hand, lived from 1903 to 1996. His life spanned the two world wars and the tremendous changes wrought by the twentieth century. It has been said that the twentieth century was the most brutal, especially in terms of its genocidal horrors. Dr. Berkouwer had much to ponder in the way of God's sovereign rule. He earned the respect of a wide spectrum of Christians in his day, and so I feel his thought is helpful for a new generation.

Finally, I want to pay tribute to my first wife, Eleanor, now with the Lord, who herself experienced major adversity, even as I was writing my earlier book, for her love and the sacrifices she made to allow me the time to study and write.

CAN YOU TRUST GOD?

And call upon me in the day of trouble;
I will deliver you, and you will honor me.

PSALM 50:15

Tragic events uncover our deepest, most personal questions about God. Many observers noted, for example, that church attendance in the United States rose just after the 9/11 terrorist attacks. People were looking for answers. Whether the difficulty is large or small, whether it strikes us personally or unfolds unemotionally on our TV screen, we tend to look for answers to our most profound questions in times of adversity.

Of course, some people are dismissive of God, even expressing anger at Him. Soon after the South Asian tsunami on December 26, 2004, a commentator in *The Herald* of Glasgow, Scotland wrote:

God, if there is a God, should be ashamed of himself.
The sheer enormity of the Asian tsunami disaster, the

death, destruction, and havoc it has wreaked, the scale of
misery it has caused, must surely test the faith of even
the firmest believer. . . . I hope I am right that there is no
God. For if there were, then he'd have to shoulder the
blame. In my book, he would be as guilty as sin and I'd
want nothing to do with him.[1]

An online poll that ran for many months following the tsunami
on the website beliefnet.com asked the following question: "Does
God have a role in natural disasters like the tsunami?" The results
consistently showed that almost half of those polled agreed with
this statement: "Although I believe in God, the supernatural had
nothing to do with this tragedy."[2]

But just as headline news raises questions about God's involvement, so does personal tragedy—perhaps even more so, because we
often suffer alone with our questions and anxieties. While writing
this chapter, I had seven friends who were battling cancer. Over
lunch one day, a businessman friend confided that his company is
perilously close to bankruptcy; another experienced heartache over
a spiritually rebellious teenager. The truth is, all of us face adversity
in various forms and at different times. One of the best-selling books
in recent years, written by a psychiatrist, put it very well with this
simple opening statement: "Life is difficult." In fact, sometimes life is
downright painful.

Adversity with its accompanying emotional pain comes in
many forms. There may be the heartache of an unhappy marriage,
or the disappointment of a miscarried pregnancy, or grief over a
spiritually indifferent or rebellious child. There is the anxiety of the
family breadwinner who has just lost his job and the despair of the
young mother who has learned she has a terminal illness.

Others experience the frustration of dashed hopes and unful-filled dreams: a business that turned sour or a career that never developed. Still others experience the sting of injustice, the dull ache of loneliness, and the stabbing pain of unexpected grief. There is the humiliation of rejection by others, the smoldering hurt of racial bias, the pain and confusion of demotion at work, and some-times worst of all, the anguish of failure that is one's own fault. Finally, there is the despair of realizing that some difficult circum-stances—a physical infirmity of your own or perhaps a severely handicapped child—will never change.

All of these circumstances and scores more contribute to the anxiety and emotional pain we all experience at various times and in varying degrees. Some pain is sudden, traumatic, and devastat-ing. Other adversities are chronic, persistent, and seemingly designed to wear down our spirits over time.

In addition to our own emotional pains, we often are called upon to help bear the pain of others, either friends or relatives. None of the illustrations I've used in the preceding paragraphs are just imaginary. I could put names alongside each one. Most of them are on my personal prayer list. When friends and loved ones hurt, we hurt.

In such days when we are struck by personal adversity—or when massive crises appear on our television screens—even the Christian is tempted to ask, "Where is God? Doesn't He care about the thousands who are starving in East Africa or the innocent civil-ians who are being brutally murdered in many war-ravaged coun-tries around the world? Doesn't He care about *me*?"

On a much smaller scale, those whose lives are free from major pain still experience the frequently frustrating or anxiety-producing events of daily life, which momentarily grab our attention and rob us of our peace of mind. A long-planned vacation has to be cancelled because of illness, the washing machine breaks down the day company arrives, your class notes are lost or stolen the day before a major exam, you tear your favorite dress on the way to church, and on and on. Instances of this magnitude are numerous. Life is full of them.

It is true that such mundane events are only temporary and pale into insignificance alongside the truly tragic events of life. Yet for most of us, life is filled with such little events, little frustrations, little anxieties, and little disappointments that tempt us to fret, fume, and worry. In the crucible of even this minor level of adversity, we are tempted to wonder, "Can I trust God?"

Even when life seems to be going our way and our daily path seems pleasant and smooth, we do not know what the future holds. As King Solomon said, "[We] do not know what a day may bring forth" (Proverbs 27:1). Someone has described life as like having a thick curtain hung across one's path, a curtain that recedes before us as we advance, but only step by step. None of us can tell what is beyond that curtain; none of us can tell what events a single day or hour may bring into our lives. Sometimes the receding curtain reveals events much as we had expected them; often it reveals events most unexpected and frequently most undesired. Such events, unfolding in ways contrary to our desires and expectations, often fill our hearts with anxiety, frustration, heartache, and grief.

People who follow Christ are not immune to such pain. In fact, it often seems as if their pain is more severe, more frequent, more unexplainable, and more deeply felt than that of the unbeliever. The problem of pain is as old as the history of man and just as universal. Even creation itself, Paul tells us, has been subjected to frustration and groans as in the pain of childbirth (see Romans 8:20-22).

So the question naturally arises, "Where is God in all of this?" Can you really trust God when adversity strikes and fills your life with pain? Does He indeed come to the rescue of those who seek Him? Does He, as the text at the beginning of this chapter affirms, deliver those who call upon Him in the day of trouble? Does the Lord's unfailing love surround the person who trusts in Him? (see Psalm 32:10).

Is God really in control? Is He trustworthy? Will He help? Even the apostle Paul pleaded with God three times to take away the thorn in his flesh before he finally found God's grace to be sufficient. Joseph pleaded with Pharaoh's cupbearer to "get me out of this prison" (Genesis 40:14). And the writer of Hebrews very honestly states, "No discipline seems pleasant at the time, but painful" (Hebrews 12:11). During the time I was working on this book I experienced one of those periods of adversity when I found it difficult to trust God. Mine happened to be a physical ailment that exacerbated a lifelong infirmity. It came at a very inconvenient time and for several weeks would not respond to any medical treatment.

During those weeks, as I continually prayed to God for relief, I was reminded of Solomon's words, "Consider what God has done: Who can straighten what he has made crooked?" (Ecclesiastes 7:13). God had brought a "crooked" event into my life, and I became acutely aware that only He could straighten it. Could I trust God whether or not He straightened my "crook" and relieved my distress? Did I really believe that a God who loved me and knew what was best for me was in control of my situation? Could I trust Him even if I didn't understand?

Further, could I encourage others to trust Him when they are in the throes of emotional pain? Is the whole idea of trusting God in adversity merely a Christian shibboleth that doesn't stand up in the face of the difficult events of life? Can you really trust God? Can you know He is in control of your particular situation? Does He care?

I have spent a good portion of my adult life encouraging people to pursue holiness, to obey God. Yet, I acknowledge that it often seems more difficult to trust God than to obey Him. The moral will of God given to us in the Bible is rational and reasonable. The circumstances in which we must trust God often appear irrational and inexplicable. The law of God is readily recognized to be good for us, even when we don't want to obey it. Yet the circumstances of our lives frequently appear to be dreadful and grim, or perhaps even calamitous and tragic. Obeying God is worked out within well-defined boundaries of God's revealed will. But trusting God is worked out in an arena that has no boundaries. We do not know the extent, the duration, or the frequency of the painful, adverse circumstances in which we must frequently trust God. We are always coping with the unknown.

Yet it is just as important to trust God as it is to obey Him. When we disobey God we defy His authority and despise His holiness. But when we fail to trust God, we doubt His sovereignty and question His goodness. In both cases we cast aspersions upon His majesty and His character. God views our distrust of Him as seriously as He views our disobedience. When the people of Israel were hungry they spoke against God, saying, "Can God spread a table in the desert? . . . Can he supply meat for his people?" The next two verses tell us, "When the LORD heard them, he was very angry . . . for they did not believe in God or trust in his deliverance" (Psalm 78:19-22).

Here's the important point: In order to trust God, we must

always view our adverse circumstances through the eyes of faith, not of sense. And just as the faith of salvation comes through hearing the message of the gospel (see Romans 10:17), so the faith to trust God in adversity comes through the Word of God alone. It is only in the Scriptures that we find an adequate view of God's relationship to and involvement in our painful circumstances. It is only from the Scriptures, applied to our hearts by the Holy Spirit, that we receive the grace to trust God in adversity.

In the arena of adversity, the Scriptures teach us three essential truths about God—truths we must believe if we are to trust Him in adversity. They are:

- God is completely sovereign.
- God is infinite in wisdom.
- God is perfect in love.

Someone has expressed these three truths as they relate to us in this way: "God in His love always wills what is best for us. In His wisdom He always knows what is best, and in His sovereignty He has the power to bring it about."

The sovereignty of God is asserted, either expressly or implicitly, on almost every page of the Bible. In my biblical research for this book, I never felt completely finished compiling the list of verses on the sovereignty of God. New references to it kept appearing almost every time I opened my Bible. We are going to look at many of these passages in later chapters, but for now consider just one:

Who can speak and have it happen
　　if the LORD has not decreed it?
Is it not from the mouth of the Most High
　　that both calamities and good things come?
　　(Lamentations 3:37-38)

This passage of Scripture offends many people. They find it difficult to accept that both calamities and good things come from God. People often ask the question, "If God is a God of love, how could He allow such a calamity?" But Jesus Himself affirmed God's sovereignty in calamity when Pilate said to Him, "Don't you realize I have power either to free you or to crucify you?" Jesus replied, "You would have no power over me if it were not given to you from above" (John 19:10-11). Jesus acknowledged God's sovereign control over His life.

Because God's sacrifice of His Son for our sins is such an amazing act of love toward us, we tend to overlook that it was for Jesus an excruciating experience beyond all we can imagine. It was for Jesus in His humanity a calamity sufficient to cause Him to pray, "My Father, if it is possible, may this cup be taken from me" (Matthew 26:39); but He did not waver in His assertion of God's sovereign control.

Rather than being offended over the Bible's assertion of God's sovereignty in both good and calamity, believers should be comforted by it. Whatever our particular calamity or adversity may be, we may be sure that our Father has a loving purpose in it. As King Hezekiah said, "Surely it was for my benefit that I suffered such anguish" (Isaiah 38:17). God does not exercise His sovereignty capriciously, but only in such a way as His infinite love deems best for us. Jeremiah wrote, "Though he brings grief, he will show compassion, so great is his unfailing love. For he does not willingly bring affliction or grief to the children of men" (Lamentations 3:32-33).

God's sovereignty is also exercised in infinite wisdom, far beyond our ability to comprehend. After surveying God's sovereign but inscrutable dealings with His own people, the Jews, the apostle Paul bows before the mystery of God's actions with these words:

Oh, the depth of the riches of the wisdom and knowledge of God! How unsearchable his judgments, and his paths beyond tracing out! (Romans 11:33)

Paul acknowledged what we must acknowledge if we are to trust God. God's plan and His ways of working out His plan are frequently beyond our ability to fathom and understand. We must learn to trust when we don't understand.

In subsequent chapters we will explore these three truths—the sovereignty, love, and wisdom of God—in greater detail. But the primary purpose of this book is not to explore these wonderful truths. The primary purpose is for us to become so convinced of these truths that we appropriate them—that we *make them our own*—in our daily circumstances; that we learn to trust God in the midst of our pain, whatever form it may take. It does not matter whether our pain is trivial or traumatic, temporary or interminable. Regardless of the nature of the circumstances, we must learn to trust God if we would glorify God in them.

But there is one final thought before we begin to explore the sovereignty, love, and wisdom of God. In order to trust God we must know Him in an intimate, personal way. David said in Psalm 9:10, "Those who know your name will trust in you, for you, LORD, have never forsaken those who seek you." To know God's name is to know Him in an intimate, personal way. It is more than just knowing facts about God. It is coming into a deeper, personal relationship with Him as a result of seeking Him in the midst of our personal pain and discovering Him to be trustworthy. It is only as we know God in this personal way that we come to trust Him. As you read the following chapters, and as you relate what you are learning about God to your own situation, pray that the Holy Spirit of God will enable you to get beyond the facts about God so that you will come to know Him better and so be able to trust Him more completely.

Discussion Questions

1. What circumstances tempt you to question whether you can trust God?
2. Which, if any, of these three statements is hardest for you to be convinced of, deep down? Why do you think that is?

    God in His love always wills what is best for us.

    In His wisdom He always knows what is best.

    In His sovereignty He has the power to bring it about.
3. Why is it so important to learn to trust God, not just obey him? You might refer to Psalm 32:10; Proverbs 3:5-8; Hebrews 11:6; or other Scripture passages in this chapter.
4. Consider keeping a journal as you read this book. Record all the circumstances in which you see God's control and guidance in your life. Ask God to open your eyes and ears to notice them. (Will you write down only pleasant circumstances?) Beginning this log now will help you see concrete evidence for truths in later chapters.

IS GOD REALLY
IN CONTROL?

God . . . is the blessed controller of all things, the
king over all kings and the master of all masters.

1 TIMOTHY 6:15, PH

Since it first appeared in 1981, the widely acclaimed book by
Rabbi Harold Kushner titled *When Bad Things Happen to Good*
People has been read by millions. The book attempts to make
sense out of a profound tragedy that occurred in the author's
family. Rabbi Kushner concludes that the writer of the book of
Job, when "forced to choose between a good God who is not
totally powerful, or a powerful God who is not totally good . . .
chooses to believe in God's goodness."[1] In Rabbi Kushner's view
of the teaching of Job, "God wants the righteous to live peace-
ful, happy lives, but sometimes even He can't bring that about.
It is too difficult even for God to keep cruelty and chaos from
claiming their innocent victims."[2]

Rabbi Kushner, of course, is not alone in his denial of the

sovereign control of God over the events of our lives. Christians as well as non-Christians frequently speak of misfortune and accidents, of circumstances beyond our (and presumably God's) control, of things just happening by chance. Down through the centuries, sickness, suffering, and sorrow have always raised questions about God's control and care of His creation.

The natural—and, on the surface at least, even logical—assumption in the minds of many is: If God is both powerful and good, why is there so much suffering, so much pain, so much heartache in the world? God is either good and not all-powerful, or He is powerful and not all good. You can't have it both ways.

The Providence of God

But the Bible teaches us that we do have it both ways. God is sovereign (all-powerful) and He is good. The Bible's teaching on this subject is categorized under a subject theologians call the Providence of God.

God's providence is a term we sometimes casually use to acknowledge God's seemingly periodic intervention in our affairs. Historically, however, the Church has always understood the providence of God to refer to His care of and governance over all of His creation at all times. Well-known theologian J. I. Packer defines providence as, "The unceasing activity of the Creator whereby, in overflowing bounty and goodwill, He upholds His creatures in ordered existence, guides and governs all events, circumstances, and free acts of angels and men, and directs everything to its appointed goal, for His own glory."[3] Note the absolute terms Packer uses: "unceasing activity," "all

events . . . all acts," "directs everything." Clearly there is no concept of now-and-then, part-time governance on God's part in
this definition.

For my own sake, I have developed a slightly shorter definition that I can more easily remember: God's providence is His
constant care for and His absolute rule over all His creation for
His own glory and the good of His people. Again, note the
absolute terms: *constant* care, *absolute* rule, *all* creation. Nothing, not even the smallest virus, escapes His care and control.

But notice also the twofold objective of God's providence:
His own glory and the good of His people. These two objec-
tives never work against each other; they are always in har-
mony. God never pursues His glory at the expense of the good
of His people, nor does He ever seek our good at the expense
of His glory. He has designed His eternal purpose so that His
glory and our good are inextricably bound together. What
comfort and encouragement this should be to us! If we are
going to learn to trust God in adversity, we must believe that
just as certainly as God will allow nothing to subvert His glory,
so He will allow nothing to spoil the good He is working out
in us and for us.

In response to our question in chapter 1—"Can you trust
God?"—the historical doctrine of God's providence clearly
affirms that we can indeed trust God. God does care for us, and
He constantly—not just occasionally—governs all the affairs of
our lives. However, as we will see in a later chapter, God's
absolute rule does not mean we are puppets without freedom of
choice and action.

But for now, let's dig a little deeper into the Bible's teaching
on God's providence. We need to consider a specific aspect of

this doctrine: the *sustaining* action of God in upholding and preserving His creation.

God Sustains

The Bible teaches that God not only created the universe, but that He upholds and sustains it day by day, hour by hour. Scripture says, "The Son is . . . sustaining all things by his powerful word" (Hebrews 1:3), and "in him all things hold together" (Colossians 1:17).

In other words, all things are indebted for their existence to the continuous sustaining action of God exercised through His Son, Jesus Christ. The so-called laws of nature are nothing more than the physical expression of the steady will of Christ. The law of gravity operates with unceasing certainty because Christ continuously wills it to operate. The stars continue in their courses because He keeps them there. Scripture says, "He . . . brings out the starry host one by one, and calls them each by name. Because of his great power and mighty strength, not one of them is missing" (Isaiah 40:26).

God's sustaining action in Christ goes beyond the inanimate creation. The Bible says that He gives life to everything (see Nehemiah 9:6). "He supplies the earth with rain and makes grass grow on the hills. He provides food for the cattle and for the young ravens when they call" (Psalm 147:8-9). God did not simply create and then walk away. He constantly sustains what He created.

Further, the Bible teaches that God sustains you and me. "He himself gives all men life and breath and everything else. . . . 'For in him we live and move and have our being'" (Acts 17:25-28).

He supplies our daily food (see 2 Corinthians 9:10). Our times are in His hands (see Psalm 31:15). Every breath we breathe is a gift from God; every bite of food we eat is given to us from His hand; every day we live is determined by Him. Does He ever leave us to our own devices, or the whims of nature, or the malevolent acts of other people? Never! He constantly sustains, provides for, and cares for us every moment of every day. Did your car break down when you could least afford the repairs? Did you miss an important meeting because the plane you were to fly in developed mechanical problems? The God who controls the stars in their courses also controls nuts and bolts and everything on your car and on that plane you were to fly in.

When I was an infant I had a bad case of measles. The virus apparently settled in my eyes and in my right ear leaving me with monocular vision and deafness in that ear. Was God in control of that virus, or was I simply a victim of a chance childhood disease? God's moment-by-moment sustaining of His universe and everything in it leaves me no choice but to accept that the virus was indeed under His controlling hand. God was not looking the other way when that virus settled in the nerve endings of my ear and the muscles of my eyes. If we are to trust God, we must learn to see that He is continuously at work in every aspect and every moment of our lives.

God Governs

The Bible also teaches that God governs the universe, not only inanimate creation, but also the actions of all creatures, both men and animals. He is called the Ruler of all things (see 1 Chronicles 29:12), the blessed and only Ruler (see 1 Timothy 6:15), the One apart from whose will the sparrow cannot fall to the ground (see Matthew 10:29). Jeremiah asks, "Who can speak and have it happen if the Lord has not decreed it?" (Lamentations 3:37). "He does as he pleases with the powers of heaven and the peoples of the earth. No one can hold back his hand or say to him: 'What have you done?'" (Daniel 4:35). "[He] is sovereign over the kingdoms of men and gives them to anyone he wishes" (Daniel 4:17).

No one can act outside of God's sovereign will or against it. Centuries ago, Saint Augustine said, "Nothing, therefore, happens unless the Omnipotent wills it to happen: he either permits it to happen, or he brings it about himself."[4] Notice how encompassing this statement is: *nothing happens without God either permitting it or directing it to happen.*

Periodically, even godly writers have taken God off His throne. A common speculation is that God has voluntarily limited Himself to the actions of human beings in order to give them their freedom. For example, Andrew Murray wrote, "In creating man with a free will and making him a partner in the rule of the earth, *God limited himself. He made himself dependent on what man would do.* Man by his prayer would hold the measure of what God could do in blessing" (emphasis added).[5] More recently, Gregory Boyd has written:

> God simply can't override free wills whenever they might conflict with his will. Because God decided to create this kind of world, he can't ensure that his will is carried out in every situation. He must tolerate and wisely work around the irrevocable freedom of human and spirit agents.[6]

Dr. Boyd's vision is of a reactive God who must "work around" the whims of His creation, unable to ensure His will is carried out. This is not the God of "unceasing activity" who "directs everything" that Dr. Packer described. Again, the providence of God is not a now-and-then operation, as though God were watching from a distance, constantly surprised by accidents, darting in once in a while to fix things after the fact, regularly frustrated by His unruly and out-of-control creation.

Confidence in God's sovereignty in *all* that influences us is crucial to our trusting Him. *If there is a single event in all of the universe that can occur outside of God's sovereign control then we cannot trust Him.* His love may be infinite, but if His power is limited and His purpose can be thwarted, we cannot trust Him.

The apostle Paul said we can entrust our most valuable possession to the Lord. In 2 Timothy 1:12, he said, "That is why I am suffering as I am. Yet I am not ashamed, because I know whom I have believed, and *am convinced that he is able to guard what I have entrusted to him* for that day" (emphasis added). "But," someone says, "Paul is speaking there of eternal life. Without question, we can entrust our eternal destiny to God, but what about our problems in this life? They make me wonder about the sovereignty of God."

But God's sovereignty does not begin at death. His sovereign direction in our lives even precedes our births. King David wrote: "For you created my inmost being; you knit me together in my mother's womb. . . . All the days ordained for me were written in your book before one of them came to be" (Psalm 139:13,16). God rules as surely on earth as He does in Heaven. For reasons known only to Himself, God permits people to act contrary to and in defiance of His revealed will in the Bible.

However, He never permits them to act contrary to His *sovereign* will, which remains incomprehensible to us.

In support of that statement—that God never permits people to act contrary to His sovereign will—consider the following passages of Scripture:

> In his heart a man plans his course,
>> but the LORD determines his steps. (Proverbs 16:9)
> Many are the plans in a man's heart,
>> but it is the LORD's purpose that prevails.
>>> (Proverbs 19:21)

> Consider what God has done:
> Who can straighten
>> what he has made crooked? (Ecclesiastes 7:13)
> Who can speak and have it happen
>> if the LORD has not decreed it? (Lamentations 3:37)
> You ought to say, "If it is the Lord's will, we will live
>> and do this or that." (James 4:15)

We make plans, but those plans can succeed only when they are consistent with God's purpose. No plan can succeed against Him. No one can straighten what He makes crooked or make crooked what He has made straight. No emperor, king, supervisor, teacher, or coach can speak and have it happen if the Lord has not first decreed to either make it happen or permit it to happen. No one can say, "I will do this or that," and have it happen if it is not part of God's sovereign will.

But when troubling or disastrous events do occur, they always hurt. We cannot dismiss them with the glib expression,

"God is in control." Yes, God is in control, but in His control He allows us to experience pain. That pain is very real. We hurt, we suffer. But in the midst of our suffering we can rest in the knowledge that He is sovereign.

Author Margaret Clarkson has beautifully written,

> The sovereignty of God is the one impregnable rock to which the suffering human heart must cling. The circumstances surrounding our lives are no accident: they may be the work of evil, but that evil is held firmly within the mighty hand of our sovereign God. . . . All evil is subject to Him, and evil cannot touch His children unless He permits it. God is the Lord of human history and of the personal history of every member of His redeemed family.[7]

Did another driver go through a red light, strike your car, and send you to the hospital with multiple fractures? Did a physician fail to detect your cancer in its early stages, when it would have been treatable? Did you end up with an incompetent instructor in a very important course in college, or an inept supervisor that blocked your career in business? All of these circumstances are under the controlling hand of our sovereign God, who is working them out in our lives for our good.

The Roman governor Felix left Paul in prison for over two years. Felix committed a totally unjust act because he wanted to grant a favor to the Jews (see Acts 24:27). Joseph was left in prison for two years because Pharaoh's cupbearer forgot him (see Genesis 40:14,23; 41:1). These two godly men were left to languish in prison—one because of deliberate injustice and the other because of inexcusable forgetfulness—but both of their predicaments were under the sovereign control of an infinitely wise and loving God.

The mighty Roman Empire could not crucify Jesus Christ unless God gave it that power (see Matthew 10:29; John 19:10-11). And what is true for Jesus is true for you and me. No detail of our lives is too insignificant for our heavenly Father's attention; no circumstance is so big that He cannot control it.

God or Chance?

This, then, is divine providence: God sustaining and governing His universe, bringing all events to their appointed end. This doctrine, however, is scarcely accepted among people today. Those who don't believe in God have, for the most part, ruled out both God's act of creation and His continuing providence. For many, all events are in the hands of fate, chance, or "a glorious accident."[8]

In his book, *When Bad Things Happen to Good People*, Rabbi Kushner asks, "Can you accept the idea that some things happen for no reason, that there is randomness in the universe?" Speaking of the direction a forest fire takes, he asks, "But is there a sensible explanation for why wind and weather combine to direct a forest fire on a given day toward certain homes rather than others, trapping some people inside and sparing others? Or is it just a matter of pure luck?"[9]

Elsewhere Rabbi Kushner reminds us that insurance companies refer to earthquakes, hurricanes, tornadoes, and various other natural disasters as "acts of God." Then he says, "I consider that a case of using God's name in vain. I don't believe that an earthquake that kills thousands of innocent victims without reason is an act of God. It is an act of nature. Nature is morally blind, without values. It churns along, following its own laws, not caring who or what gets in the way."[10]

Randomness, luck, chance, fate. This is our modern answer to the age-old question, "Why?" Of course, if one dismisses the whole idea of God, as many do, then there is no other alternative. Others, while not dismissing the idea of God, have invented a God of their own speculation. Seventeenth-century "deism" constructed a God who created a universe and then walked away to leave it running according to its natural laws and man's devices. Many of us today—even some followers of Christ—are practical "deists."

In His well-known statement about sparrows, Jesus said, "Are not two sparrows sold for a penny? Yet not one of them will fall to the ground apart from the will of your Father. . . . So don't be afraid; you are worth more than many sparrows" (Matthew 10:29-31). According to Jesus, God does exercise His sovereignty in very minute events—even in the life and death of a little sparrow. And Jesus' whole point is: If God so exercises His sovereignty in regard to sparrows, He will most certainly exercise it in regard to His children.

God's Sovereignty Is Not Always Apparent

One of our problems with the sovereignty of God is that it frequently does not appear that God is in control of the circumstances of our lives. We see unjust or uncaring or even clearly wicked people doing things that adversely affect us. We experience the consequences of other people's mistakes and failures.

We even do foolish and sinful things ourselves and suffer the often-bitter fruit of our actions.

But it is the ability of God to so arrange diverse human actions to fulfill His purpose that makes His sovereignty marvelous and yet mysterious. We have little difficulty believing that God can and has worked miracles—instances of His sovereign but *direct* intervention into the affairs of people. Regardless of our theological position regarding miracles occurring today, most of us accept without question the validity of the miracles recorded in Scripture. But to believe in the sovereignty of God when we do not *see* His direct intervention—when God is, so to speak, working entirely behind the scenes through ordinary circumstances and ordinary actions of people—is even more important, because that is the way God usually works.

A nineteenth-century writer, Alexander Carson, in his book, *Confidence in God in Times of Danger*, says, "For the wisdom of man cannot see how the providence of God can arrange human actions to fulfill his purpose without any miracle."[11] None of us knows how many times we have been unknowingly spared from adversity or tragedy by the unseen sovereign hand of God—perhaps hundreds of times. As the psalmist said, "He will not let your foot slip—he who watches over you will not slumber; indeed, he who watches over Israel will neither slumber nor sleep" (Psalm 121:3-4).

Philip Hughes writes, "Under God, however, all things are without exception fully controlled—despite all appearances to the contrary."[12] Nothing is too large or small to escape God's governing hand. The spider building its web in the corner and Napoleon marching his army across Europe are both under God's control.

Just as God's rule is invincible, so it is incomprehensible. It remains in mystery. His ways are higher than our ways (see Isaiah 55:9). His judgments are unsearchable, and His paths are beyond tracing out (see Romans 11:33). The sovereignty of God is often questioned because man *does not understand* what God is doing. And, because He does not act as we think He should, we conclude He *cannot* act for our best.

Good but Not Sovereign?

In the midst of excruciating pain, our lurking suspicion is that God is not around. When Jesus waited three days to travel to Bethany after His friend Lazarus died, Lazarus's sister Martha met Jesus with these words: "Lord, if you had been here, my brother would not have died" (John 11:21). But Jesus was fully aware of the situation. He had a deeper, more glorious purpose in mind—in this instance, resurrection.

In thinking out God's apparent absence, we can imagine that He is surprised by chance events or even frustrated by His seeming limitations. As quoted at the beginning of this chapter, Rabbi Kushner wrote that sometimes "it is too difficult even for God to keep cruelty and chaos from claiming their innocent victims."[13] This would mean God is good but not sovereign.

To corral our anxious speculation about God in times of suffering, we must shape our vision of God by the Bible, not by our experiences. The Bible leaves us no doubt: God is never frustrated. "No one can hold back his hand or say to him: 'What have you done?'" (Daniel 4:35). It is true that God is involved in an invisible war with Satan and that the lives of God's people often are battlegrounds, as seen in the life of Job. But even then,

Satan must get permission to touch God's people. (See Job 1:12; 2:6; and Luke 22:31-32.) Even in this invisible war, God is still sovereign.

Margaret Clarkson, herself a lifelong sufferer wrote, "That God is, indeed, both good and powerful is one of the basic tenets of Christian belief."[14] We admit that we are often unable to reconcile God's sovereignty and goodness in the face of widespread tragedy or personal adversity, but we believe that, although we often do not understand God's ways, He is sovereignly at work in all of our circumstances.

G. C. Berkouwer, the respected theologian of the twentieth century who taught at the Free University of Amsterdam, acknowledged that it is not easy to believe in the doctrine of the providence of God. In his book *The Providence of God*, Berkouwer wrote:

> Raw reality assaults this comforting and optimistic confession. Could the catastrophic terrors of our century, with the improportionate sufferings they inflict on individuals, families, and peoples—could these be a reflection of the guidance of God? Does not pure honesty force us to stop seeking escape in a hidden, harmonious super-sensible world? Does not honesty tell us to limit ourselves realistically to what lies before our eyes, and, without illusions, face the order of the day?[15]

All people—believers in God as well as unbelievers—experience anxiety, frustration, heartache and disappointment. Some suffer intense physical pain and catastrophic tragedies. But what should distinguish the suffering of believers from unbelievers is the confidence that our suffering is under the control of an all-powerful and all-loving God; our suffering has meaning and purpose in God's eternal plan, and He brings or allows into our lives only what is for His glory and our good.

Discussion Questions

1. What is God's providence? How is this chapter's description of providence like or unlike what you've heard before?

2. Do you embrace this understanding of providence? Why or why not?

3. Reread Lamentations 3:37-38. How do you respond to this idea?

4. God's goals are His glory and the ultimate good of each person, including you. What evidence do you find in this chapter that God cares about your good, not just His glory?

5. What's wrong with seeing God as good but not sovereign? (If your answer is "Nothing," explain why.)

6. How has this chapter helped or not helped you trust God?

GOD'S SOVEREIGNTY OVER PEOPLE

The king's heart is in the hand of the LORD;
he directs it like a watercourse
wherever he pleases.
PROVERBS 21:1

Picture yourself in this situation: You've been working for someone all of your life, your boss has been extremely cruel, your wages have kept you below the poverty line, and you feel very downtrodden and oppressed. For all practical purposes, you are nothing more than a slave. But suddenly you are freed from that almost unbearable situation. You are free to leave and start life all over again. There is only one problem—you have no financial resources, no way to make the trip, no funds to start anew someplace else, no way to take advantage of this incredible opportunity.

So you go to your boss and ask him for money for the trip and for getting started after you reach your new location. As far-fetched as it may sound, your boss gives you the money. He doesn't just give you a little, he gives you a lot; in fact, he gives you so much he impoverishes himself.

Sounds like make-believe, doesn't it? Sounds like a child-hood happily-ever-after story, the kind that never happens in real life. Only this story did happen—not in the exact details I have used, but in principle. It's recorded for us in the Bible in the book of Exodus. You know the story: The Israelites were the cruelly oppressed people, forced to "make bricks without straw." Suddenly God intervenes in their lives and Pharaoh says, "Get out!" But the Israelites had no resources for making the journey, for starting over again; they were poverty-stricken. God had foreseen this problem, however, and had made plans to overcome it. He had said to Moses:

> "And I will make the Egyptians favorably disposed toward this people, so that when you leave you will not go empty-handed. Every woman is to ask her neighbor and any woman living in her house for articles of silver and gold and for clothing, which you will put on your sons and daughters. And so you will plunder the Egyptians." (Exodus 3:21-22)

What God promised did indeed come to pass. Exodus 12:35-36 says,

> The Israelites did as Moses instructed and asked the Egyptians for articles of silver and gold and for clothing. The Lord had made the Egyptians favorably disposed toward the people, and they gave them what they asked for; so they plundered the Egyptians.

God Prompts People

The Egyptians did something completely contrary to normal human behavior. They voluntarily and freely *gave* these hitherto downtrodden slaves what they asked for, so much so that the account says the Israelites "plundered" the Egyptians. The usual meaning of plunder is to rob or seize or take by force; yet the Egyptians actually plundered themselves because God had made them "favorably disposed" toward the Israelites.

How did God do this? We don't know. We only know what the text tells us. It is obvious that the Egyptians acted freely and voluntarily of their own wills. God, in some mysterious way, moved in their hearts so that they, of their own free choice, did exactly what He planned for them to do.

At times, all of us find ourselves and our futures seemingly in the hands of other people. Their decisions or their actions determine whether we get a good grade or a poor one, whether we are promoted or fired, whether our careers blossom or fold. Of course, we cannot overlook our own responsibility in these situations. But all of us know that even when we have done our best, we are still dependent upon the favor or frown of that teacher or boss or commanding officer.

Sometimes the decisions or actions of those in charge are benevolent and good; sometimes they are wicked or careless. Either way, they do affect us, often significantly. How are we to respond when we find ourselves seemingly in the hands of someone else, when we desperately need a favorable decision or a favorable action on that person's part? Can we trust God that He can and will work in the heart of that individual to bring about His plan for us?

Or consider the instance when someone is out to harm us— to ruin our reputation, to jeopardize our career, to rob us through identity theft, or even to destroy us in a terrorist attack: Can we trust God to intervene in the heart of that person so that he does not carry out his evil intent? According to the Bible, the answer is yes in each of these instances. We can trust God. He does sovereignly intervene in the hearts of people so that they make decisions and carry out actions that accomplish His purpose for our lives. Yet God does this in such a way that these people make their decisions and carry out their plans *by their own free and voluntary choices.*

I realize that such a bold statement about the sovereignty of God acting within the minds of people gets me into a theological sand trap. We balk at the sovereignty of God over the decisions and actions of people. Such a concept of God's sovereignty appears to destroy the free will of humans and make them mere puppets on God's stage. To find our way out of this sand trap, it is important to go back to the true source of our theology—the Bible.

Perhaps the clearest biblical statement that God does sovereignly influence the decisions of people is found in Proverbs 21:1, "The king's heart is in the hand of the LORD; he directs it like a watercourse wherever he pleases." Charles Bridges, in his exposition of Proverbs, states, "The general truth [of God's sovereignty over the hearts of all people] is taught by the strongest illustration—his uncontrollable sway upon the most absolute of all wills—the king's heart."[1]

The stubborn will of the most powerful ruler on earth is directed by God as easily as the farmer directs the flow of water in his irrigation canals. The argument, then, is from the greater to the lesser—if God controls the king's heart, surely He controls everyone else's. All must move before His sovereign influence.

We have already seen this demonstrated in the actions of the Egyptians toward the Israelites. We see it also in the account of Cyrus, king of Persia, when he issued a proclamation to allow the Jews to return to Jerusalem to rebuild the temple. Ezra 1:1 says,

> In the first year of Cyrus king of Persia, in order to
> fulfill the word of the LORD spoken by Jeremiah, *the
> LORD moved the heart of Cyrus* king of Persia to make
> a proclamation throughout his realm and to put it in
> writing. (emphasis added)

The text clearly says that King Cyrus issued the proclamation because God moved his heart. The destiny of God's people was, humanly speaking, in the hands of the most powerful monarch of that day. In reality, though, their destiny was completely in God's hand, because He had the ability to sovereignly control the decisions of that monarch.

God, speaking through the prophet Isaiah, gives us another helpful insight into His working in Cyrus's heart:

> "For the sake of Jacob my servant, of Israel my chosen,
> I summon you by name and bestow on you a title of
> honor, *though you do not acknowledge me.* . . . I will
> strengthen you, *though you have not acknowledged me.*"
> (Isaiah 45:4-5, emphasis added)

It is not necessary for a person to acknowledge God's sovereign control in his heart or even to acknowledge the existence of God. Neither the Egyptians nor Cyrus intended to obey any revealed will of God. They simply acted as their hearts directed them, but their hearts were directed by God.

We see in the New Testament as well that God moves sovereignly in people's lives. Paul said of his colaborer Titus, "I thank God, who put into the heart of Titus the same concern I have for you. For Titus not only welcomed our appeal, but he is coming to you with much enthusiasm and on his own initiative" (2 Corinthians 8:16-17). Titus's actions are attributed by Paul to both God, who put a concern for the Corinthians into Titus's heart, and to Titus, who acted with enthusiasm and on his own initiative. Titus acted freely, yet under the mysterious sovereign impulse of God.

God Restrains People

So, God moves in people's hearts to show us favor when that favor will accomplish His purpose. But God also restrains people from decisions or actions that would harm us. An incident from the life of Abraham illustrates this point.

In fear of his own life, Abraham lied about his wife, Sarah, saying she was his sister. As a result, King Abimelech moved to take Sarah as his wife. God, however, kept Abimelech from carrying out his plan. He said to Abimelech, "So I have kept you from sinning against me. That is why I did not let you touch her" (Genesis 20:6). God did not physically or circumstantially restrain Abimelech. He restrained him through his mind.

God sovereignly intervened and protected the moral purity of Sarah, who was to be the mother of the promised son of Abraham. This incident is even more amazing when we consider that Abraham had put Sarah in this difficult position through his own unbelief and sin. God did not excuse Abraham's sin, but He did not let that stop Him from intervening in Abimelech's mind to prevent the serious consequences of the sin.

However, it's possible to read these accounts merely as biblical history without relating them to our lives and our situations. But Paul said, "For everything that was written in the past was written to teach us, so that through endurance and the encouragement of the Scriptures we might have hope" (Romans 15:4). These stories are meant to teach and encourage us that God is sovereign over people, and that He exercises His sovereignty for our good.

God Directs the Ruler

We saw above how God directs the heart of even the most powerful ruler, in that case King Cyrus. As we trace the sovereignty of God through the Bible, one of the most frequent references to it concerns His sovereignty over rulers and governments. Although this subject is too large for us to treat fully in this book, we must note that God ordains rulers, and He guides their decisions and military victories and defeats.

God establishes governments for the good of all people—believer as well as nonbeliever. The apostle Paul wrote: "There is no authority except that which God has established. The authorities that exist have been established by God. . . . For [the ruler] is God's servant to do you good" (Romans 13:1-4). Admittedly, the statement "the ruler is God's servant to do us good" seems difficult when we see corruption, the abuse of power, and even persecution of our brothers and sisters in Christ around the world. We must remember again that God in His infinite wisdom and sovereignty—and for reasons known only to Himself—allows rulers to act contrary to His revealed will.

Our trust must be anchored in God, not in our particular nation's military might or security apparatus. As Psalm 20:7 says, "Some trust in chariots and some in horses, but we trust in the name of the LORD our God." Another Psalm says, "No king is saved by the size of his army; no warrior escapes by his great strength. A horse is a vain hope for deliverance; despite all its great strength it cannot save" (Psalm 33:16-17).

This does not mean that our country should discharge all our military personnel and mothball our ships and tanks. It means we should not trust in them. This applies not only to civilians but to those in uniform. In the trenches and turrets of our nation's wars, many of our service personnel have found courage and the basis for prayer in the Psalms. For example, Psalm 91:2,5 reads: "I will say of the Lord, 'He is my refuge and my fortress, my God in whom I trust.' . . . You will not fear the terror of night, nor the arrow that flies by day." As our nation seeks to defend against both nuclear holocaust and terrorist attacks, we must look in prayer and trust to the God who sovereignly determines our welfare.

Does God Permit Evil?

God does not always restrain the wicked and harmful actions of others. We see this almost daily in headline news or back-page stories, either in our own locale or across the globe. Biblically, we see this even in the account of the rebuilding of the temple. There was a period of perhaps ten years when the project was stopped due to opposition from the enemies of the Jews (see Ezra 4:6-24). We do not know why God allowed the enemies of His people to prevail at one time and restrained them at another.

It is enough to know that God can and does restrain the harmful acts of others toward us when that is His sovereign will. Furthermore, God, in His infinite wisdom and love, intends that good ultimately come from those harmful acts.

The classic, oft-quoted story of Joseph illustrates this truth so well. When Joseph's brothers decided to sell him into slavery, God did not restrain them. Neither did He restrain Potiphar's wife when she maliciously and unjustly accused him. But in God's time He turned those circumstances around. God was orchestrating the wicked acts of people exactly as He planned in order to accomplish His purpose through Joseph. In the end, Joseph could look back over all the difficult events and say to his brothers, "You intended to harm me, but God intended it for good to accomplish what is now being done, the saving of many lives" (Genesis 50:20).

Are you dependent upon your boss (or your commanding officer) for advancement in your career? God will move in the heart of your boss or commander one way or the other, depending on God's plan for you. "No one from the east or the west or from the desert can exalt a man. But it is God who judges: He brings one down, he exalts another" (Psalm 75:6-7). You can trust God in all the areas of your life where you are dependent upon the favor or frown of another person. God will move in that person's heart to carry out His will for you.

The Problem of God's Sovereignty

God is infinite in His ways as well as His being. Our finite minds simply cannot comprehend an infinite being beyond what He has expressly revealed to us. Because of this, some things about God will forever remain a mystery to us. The relationship of the sovereign will of God to the freedom and moral responsibility of people is one of those mysteries.

Basil Manly, one of the founding fathers of the Southern Baptist Convention, while commenting on this difficult subject in one of his sermons, said, "The Scriptures do not undertake to explain mysteries. They leave them unexplained. There is a difference between difficulties, and mysteries: difficulties may be removed; mysteries cannot, without a new revelation, or the bestowment of a higher intellect."[2]

Here's our stumbling block: in Psalm 50:21 God says, "You thought I was altogether like you." We tend to assume God thinks as we do. We tend to think that God can only act upon the human mind in the same way we can. We can argue, persuade, or even coerce, but we cannot move a person's will. Yet the Scriptures teach that God does move a person's will, but in such a way that the person acts freely and voluntarily.

The Bible consistently portrays people as making real choices of their own will. There is never any suggestion in Scripture of people being mindless puppets moved by divine strings. Furthermore, the choices people make are moral choices; that is, people are held accountable by God for the choices they make. The actions of Judas, Herod, and Pilate were wicked acts even though done under the sovereign appointment of God.

The Bible teaches both the sovereignty of God and the free moral choices of men with equal emphasis. Richard Fuller, the third president of the Southern Baptist Convention, said, "It is impossible for us to reject either of these great truths, and it is equally impossible for our minds to reconcile them."[3]

Another truth we must keep in mind is that God is never the author of sin. Though people's sinful intents and actions serve the sovereign purpose of God, we must never conclude that God has induced anyone to sin. "When tempted, no one should say, 'God is tempting me.' For God cannot be tempted by evil, nor does he tempt anyone; but each one is tempted when, by his own evil desire, he is dragged away and enticed" (James 1:13-14). It is frequently asserted in the Scriptures that God uses the sinful actions of men to accomplish His purposes. (See, for example, Genesis 50:20; Acts 4:27-28; Revelation 17:17.) But the fact that people's sinful intents and actions serve the sovereign purpose of God does not make God the author of their sin, nor does it make them any less answerable for their actions.

But just as we must not misconstrue God's sovereignty so as to make people mere puppets, so we must not press man's freedom to the point of limiting God's sovereignty. Professor Berkouwer helps us when he says:

> [I]n the light of Scripture, it is decisive that this creaturely freedom poses no threat or limitation to the sovereign and almighty Divine enterprise. . . . We are forced to direct ourselves to the Divine revelation which reveals to us the almighty activity of God and, at the same time, teaches human responsibility. . . . And anyone who does not take both this Divine ruling and human responsibility seriously can never rightly understand history.[4]

Our Response

How shall we respond to the fact that God is able to and does in fact move in the minds and hearts of people to accomplish His will? Our first response should be one of trust. Our careers and destinies are in His hands; not the hands of bosses, commanding officers, professors, coaches, or any other people who, humanly speaking, are in a position to affect our futures. No one can harm you or jeopardize your future apart from the sovereign will of God. Moreover, God is able to and will grant you favor in the eyes of people who are in a position to do you good.

We should then look to God in prayer in all those situations where some aspect of our futures lies in the hands of another individual. As Alexander Carson said, "If we need the protection of men, let us first ask it from God. If we prevail with him, the power of the most mighty and of the most wicked must minister to our relief."[5]

In the Old Testament story, when Queen Esther was to go before King Xerxes without being summoned—an act that would normally result in her being put to death—she asked Mordecai to gather all the Jews together to fast (and presumably to pray) that the king would grant her favor. Esther did not presume to know God's will—she said, "If I perish, I perish" (Esther 4:16)—but she knew that God controlled the king's heart.

God never allows people to make decisions about us that undermine His plan for us. God is for us; we are His children; He delights in us (see Zephaniah 3:17). And the Scripture says, "If God is for us, who can be against us?" (Romans 8:31). We can put this down as a bedrock truth: God will never allow any action against you that is not in accord with His will for you.

Words of Caution

There are some important cautions we need to consider lest we wrongly use the doctrine of God's sovereignty over people.

First, we should never use the doctrine as an excuse for our own shortcomings. If you failed to get the promotion you had hoped for, or worse yet, you are fired from your job, or fail an important exam, you need to first examine your life to see if perhaps the reason lay in your own performance. Though God rescued Abraham and Sarah from the folly of Abraham's sin, He had not obligated Himself to do so. God has not promised to work in the heart of another individual just to make up for our shortcomings.

Second, we should not allow the doctrine of God's sovereignty to cause us to respond passively to the actions of other people that affect us. We should take all reasonable steps within the will of God to protect and advance our situation. I say within the will of God, because there may be other reasons, for the sake of God's Kingdom, why we should not take those steps. But the doctrine of God's sovereignty, considered by itself, should never be used to promote passivity.

Third, we must never use the doctrine of God's sovereignty to excuse our own sinful actions or decisions that hurt another person. We must never say, "Well, I made a mistake but it's okay because God is sovereign." God is indeed sovereign in that other person's life, and He may choose to use our sinful actions to accomplish His will. But He will still hold us accountable for our harmful decisions and sinful actions.

A Scripture passage that can help us keep the doctrine of God's sovereignty in perspective is Deuteronomy 29:29, "The secret things belong to the LORD our God, but the things revealed belong to us and to our children forever, that we may follow all the words of this law." We do not know what God's sovereign will is. We do not know how He will work in the heart of another individual, whether favorably or unfavorably from our viewpoint. That is in the realm of the "secret things" that are not revealed to us. But we do know He will work to accomplish His purpose, which is ultimately for both His glory and our good.

Discussion Questions

1. How does God work in the hearts of believers and unbelievers in the following passages? Note the key words used to describe what He does.
   Joshua 11:19-20
   Daniel 1:8-10
   2 Corinthians 8:16-17

2. Read Exodus 4:21 and 8:15. Note who is responsible for Pharaoh's hard heart in each verse. How do these verses, taken side by side, portray the relationship between human freedom and God's work in our hearts?

3. How do the sinful actions of humans affect God's purposes? Consider Genesis 50:20; Acts 4:27-28; and other passages in this chapter.

4. How do you think God's sovereign work in human hearts should affect the way you . . .
   pray?
   feel?
   act?

5. What if God lets someone treat you unfairly? What if He doesn't give you favor with someone important, the way He did for Daniel? How do you respond?

GOD'S POWER OVER NATURE

Do any of the worthless idols of the nations bring rain?
Do the skies themselves send down showers?
No, it is you, O LORD our God.
Therefore our hope is in you,
for you are the one who does all this.

JEREMIAH 14:22

In September 1985, an earthquake struck Mexico City killing some 6,000 people and leaving more than 100,000 homeless. A friend of mine wanted to use the event to teach his young children a simple science lesson so he asked them, "Do you know what caused the earthquake?" He planned to answer his question with a basic explanation of fault lines and shifting rocks in the earth's crust.

His seismology lesson quickly turned into a theological discussion, however, when his eight-year-old daughter replied, "I know why. God was judging those people." Though my friend's child had jumped to an unwarranted conclusion about God's judgment, she was theologically correct in one sense. God was in control of that earthquake. Why He allowed it to happen is a question we cannot answer (and should not try to), but we can say, on the testimony of Scripture, that God did indeed allow it or cause it to happen.

God Controls the Weather

All of us are affected by the weather and the forces of nature at various times to one degree or another. Most of the time we are merely inconvenienced by weather—a delayed airplane flight, a cancelled Fourth of July picnic, or something else on that order. Frequently some people somewhere are drastically affected by the weather or the more violent forces of nature. A prolonged drought withers the farmer's crop, or a hailstorm destroys it within an hour. A tornado in Texas leaves hundreds homeless, and a typhoon in Bangladesh destroys whole villages.

Whenever we are affected by the weather—whether it is merely an inconvenience or a major disaster—we tend to regard it as nothing more than the impersonal expression of certain fixed meteorological or geological laws. A low-pressure system settles over my hometown, bringing a huge snowstorm and closing our airport the day I am to leave for a speaking engagement. Forces within the earth continually bend its crust until one day it snaps, causing a major earthquake such as the 700-mile long rift under the Indian Ocean that birthed the disastrous South Asian tsunami of 2004. Whether it is trivial or traumatic, we tend to think of the expressions of nature as "just happening" and ourselves as the "unlucky" victims of whatever nature brings forth. In practice, even Christians tend to live and think like the "deists" I mentioned in an earlier chapter, who conceived of God as the One who created the universe and then walked away to leave it running according to its own natural laws.

But God has not walked away from the day-to-day control of His creation. Certainly He has established physical laws by which He governs the forces of nature, but those laws continuously operate according to His sovereign will. One meteorologist has determined that there are over 1,400 references to weather terminology in the Bible.[1] Many of these references attribute the outworking of weather directly to the hand of God. Most of these passages speak of God's control over all weather, not just His divine intervention on specific occasions.

Consider the following Scriptures:

> He unleashes his lightning beneath the whole heaven
> and sends it to the ends of the earth. . . .
> He says to the snow, "Fall on the earth,"
> and to the rain shower, "Be a mighty downpour." . . .
> The breath of God produces ice,
> and the broad waters become frozen.
> He loads the clouds with moisture;
> he scatters his lightning through them.
> At his direction they swirl around over the face of the
>   whole earth
> to do whatever he commands them.
> He brings the clouds to punish men,
> or to water his earth and show his love.
>   (Job 37:3,6,10-13)

He covers the sky with clouds;
he supplies the earth with rain
and makes grass grow on the hills. . . .
He spreads the snow like wool
and scatters the frost like ashes.
He hurls down his hail like pebbles.
Who can withstand his icy blast?
He sends his word and melts them;
he stirs up his breezes, and the waters flow.
　　(Psalm 147:8,16-18)

"I also withheld rain from you
when the harvest was still three months away.
I sent rain on one town,
but withheld it from another.
One field had rain;
another had none and dried up." (Amos 4:7)

Note how all these Scriptures attribute all expressions of weather—good or bad—to the direct controlling hand of God. The insurance companies refer to major natural disasters as "acts of God." The truth is, all expressions of nature, all occurrences of weather, whether it be a devastating tornado or a gentle rain on a spring day, are acts of God. The Bible teaches that God controls all the forces of nature, both destructive and productive, on a continuous, moment-by-moment basis.

Whether the weather is nice or bad, we are never the victims or even the beneficiaries of the impersonal powers of nature. Our loving heavenly Father is sovereign over the weather, and He exercises that sovereignty moment by moment. As G. C.

Berkouwer stated, "The believer is never the victim of the powers of nature or fate. Chance is eliminated."[2]

Complaining or Giving Thanks

Complaining about the weather seems to be a favorite American pastime. But when we complain about the weather, we are actually complaining against God who sent us our weather. We are, in fact, sinning against God (see Numbers 11:1).

Not only do we sin against God, we also deprive ourselves of the peace that comes from recognizing our heavenly Father is in control of the weather. Alexander Carson said, "Scripture represent[s] all physical laws as having their effect from the immediate agency of Almighty Power. . . . Christians themselves, though they recognize the doctrine [of divine providence], are prone to overlook it in practice, and consequently to be deprived, in a great measure, of that advantage which a constant and deep impression of this truth is calculated to give."[3] Whether the weather merely disrupts my plans or destroys my home, I need to learn to see God's sovereign and loving hand controlling it.

The fact is, for most of us, the weather and the effects of nature are usually favorable. The tornado, the drought, even the snowstorm that delays our flight are the exception, not the rule. We tend to remember the "bad" weather and take for granted the good. However, when Jesus spoke about the weather, He spoke about the goodness of God: "He causes his sun to rise on the evil and the good, and sends rain on the righteous and the unrighteous" (Matthew 5:45).

Though God sometimes uses the weather, and other expressions of nature, as an instrument of judgment (see Amos 4:7-9),

He most often uses it as an expression of His gracious provision for His creation. Both saint and sinner alike benefit from God's gracious provision of weather. And, according to Jesus, this provision is not merely the result of certain fixed, inexorable physical laws. God controls those laws. He *causes* His sun to rise, He *sends* the rain.

God has indeed established certain physical laws for the operation of His universe; yet moment by moment those laws operate according to His direct will. Again Alexander Carson put it so well when he said, "The sun and the rain minister to the nourishment and comfort equally of the righteous and the wicked, not from the necessity of general laws, but from the immediate providence of Him who, in the government of the world, wills this result."[4]

It may seem natural for us to complain about the weather, but we should learn to give thanks for it. God, our heavenly Father, sends us each day what He deems best for all of His creation.

Natural Disasters

What about the natural disasters that occur frequently in various parts of the world? Many sensitive Christians struggle over the multitude of large-scale natural disasters around the world—an earthquake in one place, famine in another, typhoons and floods somewhere else. Thousands of people are killed, others slowly starve to death. Entire regions are devastated, crops are ruined, homes destroyed. "Why does God allow all this?" we may ask. "Why does God permit all those innocent children to starve?"

It is not wrong to wrestle with these issues, as long as we do it in a reverent and submissive attitude toward God. Indeed, to fail to wrestle with the issue of large-scale tragedy may indicate a lack of compassion toward others on our part. However, we must be careful not to, in our minds, take God off His throne of absolute sovereignty or put Him in the dock and bring Him to the bar of our judgment.

One night while working on this chapter, I watched the evening news on television. One of the top stories was about several powerful tornados that swept across central Mississippi killing seven people, injuring at least 145 more, and leaving nearly 500 families homeless. As I watched the scenes of people sifting through the rubble of what had been their homes, my heart went out to them. I thought to myself, "Some of those people undoubtedly follow Christ. What would I say to them about God's sovereignty over nature? Do I really believe it myself at a time such as this? Wouldn't it be easier to just accept Rabbi Kushner's statement that it is simply an act of nature—a morally blind nature that churns along following its own laws? Why bring God into chaos and suffering such as this?"

But God brings Himself into these events. He said in Isaiah 45:7, "I form the light and create darkness, I bring prosperity and create disaster; I, the LORD, do all these things." God Himself accepts the responsibility, so to speak, of disasters. He does more than accept the responsibility; He actually claims it. In effect, God says, "I, and I alone, have the power and authority to bring about both prosperity and disaster, both weal and woe, both good and bad."

This is a difficult truth to accept as you watch people sift through the rubble of their homes or—more to the point—if you are the one sifting through the rubble of *your* home. But as

Dr. Edward J. Young commented on Isaiah 45:7, "We gain nothing by seeking to minimize the force of the present verse."[5] We must allow the Bible to say what it says, not what we think it ought to say.

We obviously do not understand why God creates disaster, or why He brings it to one town and not to another. We recognize, too, that just as God sends His sun and rain on both the righteous and the unrighteous, so He also sends the tornado, or the hurricane, or the earthquake on both. I have missionary friends who were in the middle of the 1985 earthquake in Mexico City. God's sovereignty over nature does not mean that Christians never encounter the tragedies of natural disasters. Experience and observation clearly teach otherwise.

God's sovereignty over nature does mean that, whatever we experience at the hand of the weather or other forces of nature (such as plant diseases or insect infestation of our crops), all circumstances are under the watchful eye and sovereign control of our God.

Physical Afflictions

Illness and physical affliction is another area in which we struggle to trust God. Babies are born with major birth defects. Cancer strikes people who have apparently done everything possible to guard against it. Others experience continuous pain for years without any medical relief. Even those who are normally healthy and strong often experience sicknesses at the most inopportune times. Is God in control of the diseases and physical infirmities that affect us?

When God called Moses to lead the Israelites out of Egypt,

Moses protested his inadequacy, including the fact that he was slow of speech. God's reply to Moses is very instructive to us in this area of physical affliction, for God said, "Who gave man his mouth? Who makes him deaf or mute? Who gives him sight or makes him blind? Is it not I, the LORD?" (Exodus 4:11). Here God specifically ascribes to His own work the physical afflictions of deafness, muteness, and blindness. These physical afflictions are not merely the products of defective genes or birth accidents. Those things may indeed be the immediate cause, but behind them is the sovereign purpose of God. Dr. Donald Grey Barnhouse, one of the great Bible teachers of the mid-twentieth century, once said, "No person in this world was ever blind that God had not planned for him to be blind; no person was ever deaf in this world that God had not planned for that person to be deaf. . . . If you do not believe that, you have a strange God who has a universe which has gone out of gear and He cannot control it."[6]

When Jesus encountered a man blind from birth, His disciples asked Him, "Rabbi, who sinned, this man or his parents, that he was born blind?" (John 9:2). Jesus replied, "Neither this man nor his parents sinned, but this happened so that the work of God might be displayed in his life" (verse 3). Jesus didn't respond that it was merely a birth defect that caused the man's blindness. Rather, it happened in the plan of God so that God might be glorified. God was in control of that man's blindness.

This God who is the God of deafness, muteness, and blindness is also the God of cancer, arthritis, Down's syndrome, and all other afflictions that come to us or our loved ones. None of these afflictions "just happen." They are all within the sovereign will of God. Such a statement immediately brings us into the problem of pain and suffering. Why does a sovereign God who loves us allow such pain and heartache?

The answer to that question is beyond the scope of this book. Briefly, we know that all creation has been subjected to frustration because of the sin of Adam (see Romans 8:20). So we can say that the ultimate cause of all pain and suffering must be traced back to the Fall. God's "weal and woe" are not arbitrary or capricious, but His determined response to man's sin. The sovereign God who subjected creation to frustration still rules over it, pain and all. The laws of genetics and disease are as much under His control as are the laws of meteorology. My purpose is not to deal with the problem of pain theologically but to help us deal with it on the level of faith, of trust in God. The first thing we have to do in order to trust God is determine if God is in control, if He is sovereign over the physical area of our lives. If He is not—if illness and afflictions "just happen"—then, of course, there is no basis for trusting God. But if God is sovereign in this area, then we can trust Him without understanding all the theological issues involved in the problem of pain.

Childlessness

Another common arena of struggle with trusting God is in the area of childlessness. Many couples pray for years without any results for children to be born of their marriage. Here again, however, the Bible consistently affirms that God is in control. It was said of Hannah that "the LORD had closed her womb" (1 Samuel 1:5), while He opened the womb of Leah (see Genesis 29:31). Sarah, Abraham's wife, said, "The LORD has kept me from having children" (Genesis 16:2). The angel of the Lord said to Samson's mother before his birth, "You are sterile and childless, but you are going to conceive and have a son" (Judges 13:3). The angel of the Lord also said to Zechariah, "Your prayer has been heard. Your wife Elizabeth will bear you a son" (Luke 1:13).

All of these Scripture passages teach us that God controls the conception of children. In fact, Psalm 139:13 goes a step further and says that "[God] knit me together in my mother's womb." God not only controls the conception, He even superintends the formation of that little one in his or her mother's womb. Truly God exercises a sovereign and loving control over all the works of His creation, including that which happens to our physical bodies.

How then can we trust Him in the midst of the pain of affliction or disease, or the heartache of barrenness or of a child born with a major birth defect? If God is in control, why does He allow these things to happen? In chapter 1, I said that in order to trust God in adversity we must believe that God is completely sovereign, perfect in love, and infinite in wisdom. We have not yet studied the love and wisdom of God, but for now consider just one passage of Scripture.

> For men are not cast off
> by the LORD forever.
> Though he brings grief, he will show compassion,
> so great is his unfailing love.
> For he does not willingly bring affliction
> or grief to the children of men. (Lamentations 3:31-33)

God does not willingly bring affliction or grief to us. He does not delight in causing us to experience pain or heartache. He always has a purpose for the grief He brings or allows to come into our lives. Most often we do not know what that purpose is, but it is enough to know that His infinite wisdom and perfect love have determined that the particular sorrow is best for us. God never wastes pain. He always uses it to accomplish His purpose. And His purpose is for His glory and our good. Therefore, we can trust Him when our hearts are aching or our bodies are racked with pain.

Trusting God in the midst of our pain and heartache means that we *accept* it from Him. There is a vast difference between acceptance and either resignation or submission. We can resign ourselves to a difficult situation, simply because we see no other alternative. Many people do that all the time. Or we can submit to the sovereignty of God in our circumstances with a certain amount of reluctance. But to truly accept our pain and heartache has the connotation of willingness. An attitude of acceptance says that we trust God, that He loves us and knows what is best for us.

Acceptance does not mean that we do not pray for physical healing, or for the conception and birth of a little one to our marriage. We should indeed pray for those things, but we should pray in a trusting way. We should realize that, though God can do all things, for infinitely wise and loving reasons He may not do what we pray He will do. How do we know how long to pray? As long as we can pray trustingly, with an attitude of acceptance of His will, we should pray as long as the desire remains.

Many hundreds of years ago, the prophet Habakkuk struggled with the question of "Where is God?" in all the evil that he saw around him. He finally came to the conclusion that, though he did not understand what God was doing, he would trust Him. His affirmation of trust, couched in the language of a world falling apart around him, would be a fitting example for us to follow as we struggle with God's sovereignty over nature. Habakkuk said:

Though the fig tree does not bud
and there are no grapes on the vines,
though the olive crop fails
and the fields produce no food,
though there are no sheep in the pen
and no cattle in the stalls,
yet I will rejoice in the LORD,
I will be joyful in God my Savior. (Habakkuk 3:17-18)

Discussion Questions

1. What is your usual attitude toward the weather? Do you tend to complain about it? Thank God for it? Feel that God isn't involved with it on a day-to-day basis?

2. a. For what does God take responsibility in Exodus 4:11 and Isaiah 45:7?

   b. What are some possible responses to these verses?

   c. Which response do you choose? Why?

3. The idea that God claims responsibility for deadly earthquakes, droughts, blindness, and childlessness prompts sensitive people to ask questions. Are there limits to the kinds of questions we should ask God? If so, what limits? If not, why not?

4. What are some possible reasons why God leaves many of our questions unanswered?

5. The fall of humans into sin subjected all of creation to frustration and set in motion the forces that lead to droughts and disabilities. Yet God has the power to prevent any specific tragedy; so when He doesn't, He's responsible. Does that hinder you from trusting Him? Why or why not?

6. What do you make of Habakkuk 3:17-19? To what extent are you able to adopt that attitude to your circumstances?

GOD'S SOVEREIGNTY AND OUR RESPONSIBILITY

But we prayed to our God and posted a
guard day and night to meet this threat.

NEHEMIAH 4:9

There is an old story about a man who carried the doctrine of God's sovereignty to such an extreme that he drifted into a sort of divine fatalism. One day, walking down a flight of stairs, he carelessly stumbled and fell headlong to the bottom of the staircase. Picking himself up, he gingerly felt his bruises and said to himself, "Well, I'm glad that one is over."

If we are not careful, you and I can, like the foolish man in the story, drift into a fatalistic attitude about the sovereignty of God. A student who fails an important exam tries to excuse himself by saying, "Well, God is sovereign, and He determined that I should fail that exam." A driver can cause an auto accident and, in his own mind, evade his carelessness by attributing the accident to the sovereignty of God. Obviously both attitudes are unbiblical and foolish, yet we can easily drift into them.

Sovereignty and Prayer

In the last chapter we looked at God's sovereign control over the weather and other forces of nature. As a frequent air traveler, I have been affected many times by weather unsuitable for flying. One afternoon, driving home in a snowstorm, I was reflecting on the fact that our airport was closed because of the storm and that I was scheduled to leave the next morning to speak at a weekend conference. But I said to myself and to God, "God, I know that You are in control of this storm, and You are also in control of the conference I am to speak at. If You want me to be at that conference tomorrow night, You will move this storm out so our airport can reopen tomorrow morning. I'm not going to be anxious about it."

Now, I have to admit that such an attitude of refusing to be anxious was progress for me in coping with adverse flying weather. After arriving home, I announced to my wife my decision not to be anxious about whether I would be able to leave on schedule the following morning. She looked at me with a smile and said, "Don't be anxious, but pray about it."

I thought to myself, "How foolish I was." I had been concentrating so strongly on God's sovereignty over the weather that I completely neglected His express command to make a specific request. He does indeed say to us, "Do not be anxious about anything," but then immediately follows that with, "but in everything, by prayer and petition, with thanksgiving, present your requests to God" (Philippians 4:6).

God was certainly in sovereign control of the snowstorm that had closed our airport. But the knowledge of His sovereignty is meant to be an encouragement to pray, not an excuse to lapse into a sort of pious fatalism.

The fourth chapter of Acts tells about Peter and John being threatened by the Jewish Sanhedrin and commanded not to speak or teach at all in the name of Jesus. When Peter and John reported this to the other believers they raised their voices together in prayer:

> "Sovereign Lord," they said, "you made the heaven and the earth and the sea, and everything in them. . . .
> They [Herod, Pontius Pilate, the Gentiles, and Jews] did what your power and will had decided beforehand should happen. Now, Lord, consider their threats and enable your servants to speak your word with great boldness." (Acts 4:24,28-29)

The disciples believed in the sovereignty of God. But God's sovereignty to them was a reason and an encouragement to pray. They believed because God was sovereign He was able to answer their prayers. They acknowledged God's sovereign purpose in events past (i.e., the Crucifixion), but they did not presume to know the divine decree about future events. They only knew Christ had commanded them to be His witnesses in Jerusalem, and in all Judea and Samaria, and to the ends of the earth. So they prayed, confident that the sovereign God, who had commanded them to be witnesses, was able to clear away the obstacles to their obedience.

Prayer assumes the sovereignty of God. If God is not sovereign, we have no assurance that He is able to answer our prayers. Our prayers would become nothing more than wishes. But while God's sovereignty, along with His wisdom and love, is the foundation of our trust in Him, prayer is the expression of that trust.

The Puritan preacher Thomas Lye, in a sermon entitled "How Are We to Live by Faith on Divine Providence?" said, "As prayer without faith is but a beating of the air, so trust without prayer [is] but a presumptuous bravado. He that promises to give, and bids us trust his promises, commands us to pray, and expects obedience to his commands. He will give, but not without our asking."[1]

The apostle Paul, while imprisoned in Rome, wrote to his friend Philemon, "Prepare a guest room for me, because I hope to be restored to you in answer to your prayers" (Philemon 22). Paul did not presume to know God's secret will. He *hoped* to be restored. He did not say, "I will be restored." But he did know that God in His sovereignty was well able to effect his release, so he asked Philemon to pray. Prayer was the expression of his confidence in the sovereignty of God.

John Flavel was another Puritan preacher and a prolific writer (six volumes of collected works). He wrote a classic treatise entitled *The Mystery of Providence*, first published in 1678.[2] It is instructive to note that Flavel begins this treatise on the sovereign providence of God with a discourse on Psalm 57:2, "I cry out to God Most High, to God, who fulfills his purpose for me." That is, Flavel says to us, because God is sovereign, we should pray. God's sovereignty does not negate our responsibility to pray, but rather makes it possible to pray with confidence.

Sovereignty and Prudence

Just as God's sovereignty does not set aside our responsibility to pray, it also does not negate our responsibility to act prudently. To act prudently, in this context, means to use all legitimate, biblical means at our disposal to avoid harm to ourselves or others and to bring about what we believe to be the right course of events.

An illustration of using all proper means to avoid harm is seen in the life of David as he continually evaded Saul while Saul was determined to kill him. David had already been anointed to succeed Saul as king (see 1 Samuel 16:13). And as we have just seen in Psalm 57:2, David was confident that God would fulfill His purpose for him. Yet David took all the precautions he could to avoid being killed by Saul. He did not presume upon the sovereignty of God but rather acted prudently in dependence upon God to bless his efforts.

We see in Paul's life an illustration of prudent action to bring about the right course of events. The story involves Paul's trip to Rome and the shipwreck that occurred on the island of Malta, recorded in Acts 27. After many days of being battered by a storm of hurricane force, and when everyone had given up all hope of being saved, Paul stood before them and said:

> But now I urge you to keep up your courage, because
> not one of you will be lost; only the ship will be
> destroyed. Last night an angel of the God whose I am
> and whom I serve stood beside me and said, "Do not
> be afraid, Paul. You must stand trial before Caesar; and
> God has graciously given you the lives of all who sail

with you." So keep up your courage, men, for I have
faith in God that it will happen just as he told me.
Nevertheless, we must run aground on some island.
(Acts 27:22-26)

Paul not only trusted in the sovereignty of God, he had an
express revelation from heaven that no life would be lost in the
shipwreck. Yet some time later, when he saw the sailors trying
to escape from the ship with the lifeboat, he said to the Roman
centurion, "Unless these men stay with the ship, you cannot be
saved" (Acts 27:31). Paul apparently realized that the presence
of the skilled sailors was necessary for the safety of the passen-
gers, even at that point. Therefore, he took prudent action to
bring about that which God by divine revelation had already
promised would certainly come to pass. He did not confuse
God's sovereignty with his responsibility to act prudently.

Paul did not consider God's sovereign purpose a reason to
neglect his duty even though, in that instance, God's purpose
had been revealed to him by an angel from heaven. In our circumstances today, we do not know what God's sovereign purpose is in a specific situation. We should be even more aware
not to use God's sovereignty as an excuse to shirk the duties that
He has commanded in the Scriptures. God usually works through
means, and He intends that we use the means He has placed at
our disposal.

When Nehemiah was rebuilding the wall around Jerusalem,
he and his people faced the threat of an armed attack from their
enemies (see Nehemiah 4:7-8). Nehemiah's response was to pray
and post a guard—prayer and prudence (see verse 9). In addition
the text says, "From that day on, half of my men did the work,

while the other half were equipped with spears, shields, bows and armor." Not only that but, "Those who carried materials did their work with one hand and held a weapon in the other, and each of the builders wore his sword at his side as he worked" (verses 16-18).

Nehemiah trusted in the sovereignty of God. He said, "Our God will fight for us!" (verse 20). But he also used all available means, believing that God in His sovereignty would bless those means.

One of the most basic means of prudence that God has given to us is prayer. We must not only pray for His overruling providence in our lives as David did (see Psalm 57:2), but we must also pray for wisdom to rightly understand our circumstances and use the means He has given us. When the Gibeonites sought to deceive Joshua and the men of Israel, they came with worn clothing and dried-out bread, pretending to have come from far away. The Scripture says, "The men of Israel sampled their provisions but did not inquire of the LORD" (Joshua 9:14). As a result they were deceived by the Gibeonites and made a treaty with them, when they should have destroyed them. They were not prudent because they did not pray and ask God for wisdom and insight to understand the situation.

Another means of prudence God has given us is the opportunity to seek wise and godly counsel. Proverbs 15:22 says, "Plans fail for lack of counsel, but with many advisers they succeed." However, Proverbs 16:9 tells us that a person's plans succeed only within the sovereign will of God. All the wise counsel in the world cannot enable our plans to succeed contrary to the sovereign will of God. But God uses the wise counsel of others to bring our plans into line with His sovereign will. Once again,

we must not confuse duty—in this case, to seek wise counsel—
with God's sovereign will.

Prayer and Prudence

Earlier, I referred briefly to Nehemiah's use of prayer and prudence, "But we prayed to our God and posted a guard day and
night to meet this threat" (Nehemiah 4:9). Prayer is the
acknowledgment of God's sovereignty and of our dependence
upon Him to act on our behalf. Prudence is the acknowledgment of our responsibility to use all legitimate means. We must
not separate these two. We see this beautifully illustrated for us
in the following passage of Scripture:

> The Reubenites, the Gadites and the half-tribe of Man-
> asseh had 44,760 men ready for military service—able-
> bodied men who could handle shield and sword, who
> could use a bow, and who were trained for battle. They
> waged war against the Hagrites, Jetur, Naphish and
> Nodab. They were helped in fighting them, and God
> handed the Hagrites and all their allies over to them,
> because they cried out to him during the battle. He
> answered their prayers, because they trusted in him.
> (1 Chronicles 5:18-20)

The warriors described in this passage were able-bodied and
well-trained. They were prudent; they had taken all precautions
to be able to fight when they needed to. But they did not trust in
their ability and training. They cried out to God, and He answered
their prayers because they trusted in Him. God sovereignly

intervened. He handed all their enemies over to them because they prayed.

All of our plans, all of our efforts, and all of our prudence is of no avail unless God prospers those means. Psalm 127:1 says, "Unless the LORD builds the house, its builders labor in vain. Unless the LORD watches over the city, the watchmen stand guard in vain." In this passage there is the concept of both offensive and defensive efforts—of both building for progress and watching against destruction. In a sense, the verse sums up all of our responsibilities in life. Whether it be in the physical, the mental, or the spiritual, we should always be building and watching. And Psalm 127:1 says none of those efforts will prosper unless God intervenes in them.

Note how strongly the psalmist described the necessity of God's intervention in our efforts. He does not say, "Unless God *blesses* or *helps* the builders and the watchmen, their efforts are in vain." Rather he speaks in terms of God Himself building the house and watching over the city. At the same time, there is, of course, no suggestion in the text that God *replaces* the builders and the watchmen. The obvious meaning is that in every respect we are dependent upon God to enable us and prosper our efforts.

We must depend upon God to do *for* us what we cannot do for ourselves. We must, to the same degree, depend on Him to *enable* us to do what we must do for ourselves. The farmer must use all of his skills, experience, and resources to produce a harvest. Yet he is utterly dependent upon forces outside of himself. Those forces of nature—moisture, insects, sun—are, as we have already seen, under the direct sovereign control of God. The farmer is dependent upon God to control nature so that his crop will grow. But he is just as dependent upon God to enable him to plow, plant, fertilize, and cultivate properly. From where did he get his skills, his ability to learn from his experience, the financial resources to buy the equipment and fertilizer he uses? Where does even his physical strength to do his tasks come from? Are not all these things from the hand of God who "gives all men life and breath and everything else" (Acts 17:25)? In every respect, we are utterly dependent upon God.

There are times when we can do nothing, and there are times when we must work. In both instances we are equally dependent upon God. When the Israelites were in the desert, they were consciously dependent upon God for both food and water. Moses said to them, "He humbled you, causing you to hunger and then feeding you with manna . . . to teach you that man does not live on bread alone but on every word that comes from the mouth of the LORD" (Deuteronomy 8:3). The Israelites had to learn that they could not simply dig into their food supplies to eat whenever they desired. God reduced them to a conscious dependence upon His daily provision.

The time would come, however, when they would be in "a land where bread will not be scarce and you will lack nothing" (Deuteronomy 8:9). Then, Moses warned them, they were not to trust in their own ability as farmers, saying to themselves, "My power and the strength of my hands have produced this wealth for me." Rather he warned them to "remember the LORD your God, for it is he who gives you the ability to produce wealth" (Deuteronomy 8:17-18).

Sometimes, God reduces us to a *conscious*, utter dependence upon Him. A loved one is desperately ill, beyond the expertise and skill of medical service. Unemployment has persisted to the point that the cupboard is bare and no job prospects are in sight. At such times we readily recognize our dependence and cry out to God for His intervention. But we are just as dependent on God when the physician diagnoses a routine illness and prescribes a successful medication. We are just as dependent when the paycheck comes regularly and all our material needs are met.

At the same time we are responsible. The Bible never allows us to use our utter dependence on God as an excuse for indolence. Ecclesiastes 10:18 says, "If a man is lazy, the rafters sag; if his hands are idle, the house leaks." And again, "A sluggard does not plow in season; so at harvest time he looks but finds nothing" (Proverbs 20:4). We are absolutely dependent upon God but, at the same time, we are responsible to diligently use whatever means are appropriate for the occasion.

The man in our story at the beginning of the chapter should have been more careful walking down the stairs. He might have paid attention to the "please use the handrail" notice. He cannot blame a divine fatalism for his fall. Neither can the student who fails her exam, nor the worker who loses his job for lack of diligence, nor the person who becomes ill because of poor health habits. Our *duty* is found in the *revealed* will of God in the Scriptures. Our *trust* must be in the *sovereign* will of God, as He works in the ordinary circumstances of our daily lives for our good and His glory.

There is no conflict between trusting God and accepting our responsibility. Thomas Lye, the Puritan preacher quoted earlier in the chapter, said, "Trust . . . [uses] such means as God prescribes for the bringing about his appointed end. . . . God's means are to be used, as well as God's blessing to be expected."[3]

And Alexander Carson made a similar observation when he

said, "Let us learn . . . that as God has promised to protect us and provide for us, it is through the means of his appointment, vigilance, prudence, and industry, that we are to look for these blessings."[4]

Our Failures and God's Sovereignty

We have seen that God's sovereignty does not do away with our duty to act responsibly and prudently on all occasions. But what about the other side of the question? Does failure on our part to act prudently frustrate the sovereign plan of God? The Scriptures never indicate that God is frustrated to any degree by our failure to act as we should. In His infinite wisdom, God's sovereign plan includes our failures and even our sins.

When Mordecai asked Queen Esther to intercede with King Xerxes on behalf of the Jews, she demurred with the explanation that she could enter the king's presence unbidden only on the threat of death (Esther 4:10-11). However, Mordecai sent word back to her, "For if you remain silent at this time, relief and deliverance for the Jews will arise from another place, but you and your father's family will perish. And who knows but that you have come to royal position for such a time as this?" (Esther 4:14). The key phrase in Mordecai's response is "relief and deliverance for the Jews will arise from another place."

God, in His infinite wisdom and resources, was not limited to Esther's response. The options available to God to bring about deliverance for the Jews were as infinite as His wisdom and power. He literally did not need Esther's cooperation. But in this instance, He chose to use her. Mordecai's closing argument to Esther, "And who knows but that you have come to royal position for such a time as this?" assumes that God uses people and means to accomplish His sovereign purpose.

As subsequent events proved, God had indeed raised up Esther to accomplish His purpose. But He could just as easily have raised up someone else or used an altogether different means. God usually works through ordinary events (as opposed to miracles) and the voluntary actions of people. But He always provides the means necessary and guides them by His unseen hand. He is sovereign, and He cannot be frustrated by our failure to act or by our actions, which in themselves are sinful. We must always remember, however, that God still holds us accountable for the very sins that He uses to accomplish His purpose.

As we conclude these studies on God's sovereignty and turn our attention to His wisdom and love, we need to realize once again that there is no conflict in the Bible between His sovereignty and our responsibility. Both concepts are taught with equal force and with never an attempt to "reconcile" them. Let us hold equally to both, doing our duty as it is revealed to us in the Scriptures and trusting God to sovereignly work out His purpose in us and through us.

Discussion Questions

1. Read Acts 27:13-44. What relationship does this story show between God's sovereignty and our responsibility?

2. Read Psalm 127:1. How is the Lord involved in something you are building (such as a business, a house, a relationship, a family)?

3. In Nehemiah 4:6-9, what is the relationship between prayer and prudence?

4. When we trust God and have a peace that comes from Him alone, our prayers are different from prayers that flow out of anxiety. How are they different?

5. a. If God is in control and His purpose will inevitably prevail, why do we need to pray?

   b. Why do we need to make every effort to act with wisdom?

6. Choose a difficult situation for which you are presently praying. Write a prayer for that situation from a mind-set of trust. (If you are meeting with a group, you might pray for one another about these situations.)

THE WISDOM OF GOD

*Oh, the depth of the riches of the
wisdom and knowledge of God!
How unsearchable his judgments,
and his paths beyond tracing out!*

ROMANS 11:33

"At 9:15 a.m., just after the children had settled into their first lesson on the morning of 21 October 1966, a waste tip from a South Wales [coal mine] slid into the quiet mining community of Aberfan. Of all the heart-rending tragedies of that day, none was worse than the fate of the village junior school. The black slime slithered down the man-made hillside and oozed its way into the classrooms. Unable to escape, five teachers and 109 children died.

"A clergyman being interviewed by a B.B.C. reporter at the time of [the tragedy, in response] . . . to the inevitable question about God [said], 'Well. . . I suppose we have to admit that this is one of those occasions when the Almighty made a mistake.'"[1]

In a time of disaster, even the most saintly among us is tempted to blurt out blasphemy. When calamity of some kind strikes us, we wonder if God hasn't made a mistake. I think of another statement—not flippant, but heartfelt—made by a sincere Christian watching a child struggle with cancer, "I sure hope God knows what He's doing in this." Anyone who has dealt deeply with adversity can probably identify with the doubts this person struggled with.

When we stop and think about it, we know in our heart of hearts that God does not make any mistakes in our lives or the villages of South Wales or anywhere else. God does know what He is doing. God is infinite in His wisdom. He always knows what is best for us and what is the best way to bring about that result.

Wisdom is commonly defined as good judgment, or the ability to develop the best course of action, or the best response to a given situation. We all recognize that human wisdom at its best is fallible. The wisest men or women simply do not have all the facts of a given situation, nor are they able to predict with certainty the results of a given course of action. All of us from time to time agonize over some important decisions, trying to determine the best course of action.

But God never has to agonize over a decision. He does not even have to deliberate within Himself or consult others outside of Himself. His wisdom is intuitive, infinite, and infallible: "His understanding has no limit" (Psalm 147:5).

Nineteenth-century theologian J. L. Dagg described wisdom as "consisting in the selection of the best end of action, and the adoption of the best means for the accomplishment of this end." He then said, "God is infinitely wise, because he selects the best possible end of action . . . [and] because he adopts the best possible means for the accomplishment of the end which he has in view."[2]

The best possible end of all of God's actions is ultimately His glory. That is, all that God does or allows in all of His creation will ultimately serve His glory. As John Piper says in his book *Desiring God*, "The chief end of *God* is to glorify God and enjoy himself forever."[3] One has only to thumb through the New Testament looking at passages with the word *glory* in them to agree with John Piper that the chief end of God is His own glory. (Just for starters look up John 15:8; Romans 1:21; 11:36; 1 Corinthians 10:31; Ephesians 1:12,14; Revelation 4:11; 5:13; 15:4.)

Beauty Out of Ashes

As we watch tragic events unfold, or more particularly as we experience adversity ourselves, we often are prone to ask God, "Why?" The reason we ask is because we do not see any possible good to us or glory to God that can come from the particular adverse circumstances that have come upon us or our loved ones. But is not the wisdom of God—thus the glory of God—more eminently displayed in bringing good out of calamity than out of blessing?

There is no question that God's people live in a hostile world. We have an enemy, the Devil, who "prowls around like a roaring lion looking for someone to devour" (1 Peter 5:8). He wants to sift us like wheat as he did Peter (see Luke 22:31), or make us curse God as he tried to get Job to do. God does not spare us from the ravages of disease, heartache, and disappointment of this sin-cursed world. But God is able to take all of these elements—the bad as well as the good—and make full use of everything and everyone.

As someone said years ago,

> A lesser wisdom than the Divine would feel impelled
> to forbid, to circumvent or to resist the outworking of
> these hellish plans. It is a fact that often God's people
> try to do this themselves, or cry unceasingly to the Lord
> that He may do it. So it is that prayers often seem to lie
> unanswered. For we are being handled by a wisdom
> which is perfect, a wisdom which can achieve what it
> [intends] by taking hold of things and people which
> are meant for evil and making them work together for
> good.[4]

God's infinite wisdom then is displayed in bringing good out of evil, beauty out of ashes. It is displayed in turning all the forces of evil that rage against His children into good for them. But the good that He brings about is often different from the good we envision.

Holiness Out of Adversity

Romans 8:28, "And we know that in all things God works for the good of those who love him, who have been called according to His purpose," is an oft-quoted verse. But we often fail to note that the following verse helps us understand what the "good" of verse 28 is. Verse 29 begins with the word *for*, indicating that it is a continuation and amplification of the thought of verse 28. It says, "For those God foreknew he also predestined to be conformed to the likeness of his Son, that he might be the firstborn among many brothers."

The good that God works for in our lives is conformity to the likeness of His Son. So, His good is *not necessarily our present comfort or happiness but rather conformity to Christ* in ever-increasing measure for eternity.

We see this same thought in Hebrews 12:10, "Our fathers disciplined us for a little while as they thought best; but God disciplines us for our good, that we may share in his holiness." To share in God's holiness is an equivalent expression to being conformed to the likeness of Christ. God knows exactly what He intends we become and He knows exactly what circumstances, both good and bad, are necessary to produce that result in our lives.

Note the contrast the author of Hebrews draws between the finite, fallible wisdom of human parents and the infinite, infallible wisdom of God. He says, "Our fathers disciplined us for a little while as they thought best." As a father, I can readily identify with the phrase "as they thought best." Sometimes in rearing our children we agonized over the proper discipline, both in kind and amount. And even when we thought we knew what was best, there were many times when we erred.

But, the writer says without qualification, God disciplines us for our good. There is no agonizing by God, no hoping He has made the right decision, no wondering what is really best for us. God makes no mistakes. He knows infallibly with infinite wisdom what combination of good and bad circumstances will bring us more and more into sharing His holiness. He never puts too much of the "salt" of adversity into the recipe of our lives. His blending of adversity and blessing is always exactly right for us.

The author of Hebrews readily admits that discipline is painful (12:11). But he also assures us it is profitable. It produces "a harvest of righteousness and peace." The purpose of God's discipline is not to punish us but to transform us. He has already meted out punishment for our sins on Jesus at Calvary: "The punishment that brought us peace was upon him" (Isaiah 53:5). But we must be transformed more and more into the likeness of Christ. That is the purpose of discipline.

The psalmist said, "It was good for me to be afflicted so that I might learn your decrees" (Psalm 119:71). He is speaking of experiential learning. We can learn God's will for our character intellectually through reading and studying the Scriptures—and we should do that. That is where change begins, as our minds are renewed. But real change—down in the depth of our souls—is produced as the tenets of Scripture are worked out in real life. This usually involves adversity. We may admire and even desire the character trait of patience, but we will never learn patience until we have been treated unjustly and learn experientially to "suffer long" (the meaning of patience) the one who treats us unjustly.

If you stop and think about it, you will realize that *most godly character traits can only be developed through adversity*. God in His infinite wisdom knows exactly what adversity we need to grow more and more into the likeness of His Son.

God Doesn't Explain

Does God explain to us what he is doing in adversity? There is no indication that God ever explained to Job the reasons for all of his terrible sufferings. As readers, we are taken behind the scenes to observe the spiritual warfare between God and Satan, but as far as we can tell from Scripture, God never told Job about that.

The fact is, God has not really told us, even in Scripture, why He allowed Satan to so afflict Job as he did. On the basis of the truth of Romans 8:28 (which was just as valid for Job as it is for us), we must conclude that God had a much higher purpose in allowing Satan's onslaughts against Job than merely using Job as a pawn in a "wager" between Himself and Satan. The story concludes with a conversation between God and Job in which Job acknowledges that through his trials he has come into a new and deeper relationship with God. He said, "My ears had heard of you but now my eyes have seen you" (Job 42:5).

Sometimes afterward we can see some of the beneficial results of adversity in our lives, but we seldom can see it during the time of the adversity. Joseph could surely see, after he had become prime minister of Egypt, some of the results of the affliction God had allowed in his life, but he certainly could not see this while going through it. To him the whole painful process must have seemed devoid of any meaning and very contrary to his expectations of the future, as given to him through his dreams.

But whether we see beneficial results in this life or not, we are still called upon to trust God that in His love He wills what is best for us and in His wisdom He knows how to bring it about.

So we should never ask "why?" in the sense of demanding that God explain or justify His actions or what He permits in our lives. Margaret Clarkson said, "We may not demand of a sovereign Creator that He explain Himself to His creatures. . . . God had good and sufficient reasons for His actions; we trust His sovereign wisdom and love."[5]

When I say we should never ask "why?" I am not talking

about the reactive and spontaneous cry of anguish when calamity first befalls us or one we love. Rather, I am speaking of the persistent and demanding "why?" that has an accusatory tone toward God in it. The former is a natural human reaction; the latter is a sinful human reaction. Three of the psalms begin with "why": Why do you stand far off? Why have you forsaken me? Why have you rejected us forever? (Psalms 10; 22; 74). But each of those psalms ends on a note of trust in God. The psalm writers did not allow their "whys" to drag on. They did not allow them to take root and grow into accusations against God. Their "whys" were really cries of anguish, a natural reaction to pain.

God's Ways Are Incomprehensible

Sometimes we come to the place where we do not demand of God that He explain Himself, but we try to determine or comprehend for ourselves what God is doing. We are unwilling to live without rational reasons for what is happening to us or those we love. We are almost insatiable in our quest for the "why" of the adversity that has come upon us. But this is a futile as well as an untrusting task. God's ways, being the ways of infinite wisdom, simply cannot be comprehended by our finite minds.

God Himself said through Isaiah, " 'For my thoughts are not your thoughts, neither are your ways my ways,' declares the LORD. 'As the heavens are higher than the earth, so are my ways higher than your ways and my thoughts than your thoughts'" (Isaiah 55:8-9). In his commentary on Isaiah, Edward J. Young said of this passage, "The implication is that just as the heavens are so high above the earth that by human standards their height cannot be measured, so also are God's ways and thoughts so above those of man that they cannot be grasped by man in their fullness. In other words, the ways and thoughts of God are incomprehensible to man."[6]

The apostle Paul states the same truth in his doxology at the end of Romans 11 when he exclaims in amazement, "Oh, the depth of the riches of the wisdom and knowledge of God! How unsearchable his judgments, and his paths beyond tracing out!" (verse 33).

God's wisdom is fathomless; His decisions are unsearchable; His methods are mysterious and untraceable. No one has ever even understood His mind, let alone advised Him on the proper course of action. How futile and even arrogant for us to seek to determine what God is doing in a particular event or circumstance. We simply cannot search out the reasons behind His decisions or trace out the ways by which He brings those decisions to pass.

If we are to experience peace in our souls in times of adversity, we must come to the place where we truly believe that God's ways are simply beyond us and stop asking Him "why" or even trying to determine it ourselves. This may seem like an intellectual "cop out," a refusal to deal with the really tough issues of life. In fact, it is just the opposite. It is a surrender to the truth about God and our circumstances as it is revealed to us by God Himself in His inspired Word.

C. H. Spurgeon, again in his sermon on divine providence, said,

> Providence is wonderfully intricate. Ah! you want always to see through Providence, do you not? You never will, I assure you. You have not eyes good enough. You want to see what good that affliction

was to you; you must believe it. You want to see how it can bring good to the soul; you may be enabled in a little time; but you can not see it now; you must believe it. Honor God by trusting him.[7]

In Job's final response to God, he humbly acknowledges God's unfathomable ways. He says,

"You asked, 'Who is this that obscures my counsel without knowledge?' Surely I spoke of things I did not understand, things too wonderful for me to know." (Job 42:3)

God's ways, said Job, were too wonderful for him to know or understand. When he saw God in His great majesty and sovereignty, he repented of his arrogant questioning in "dust and ashes." He stopped asking and simply trusted.

Don't Interpret, but Learn!

Because God's wisdom is infinite and His ways inscrutable to us, we should also be very careful in seeking to interpret the ways of God in His providence, especially in particular events. Additionally, we need to be cautious of others who offer themselves as interpreters about the why and wherefore of all that is happening. Be wary of those who say, "God let this happen so that you might learn such and such a lesson." The fact is, we do not *know* what God is doing through a particular set of circumstances or events.

This does not mean we should not seek to learn from God's providence as well as His revealed will in Scripture. Quite the contrary. As we observed earlier in the chapter, the psalmist learned God's decrees experientially through affliction (see Psalm 119:71). The people of Israel also learned through God's adverse providence in their lives. Deuteronomy 8:3 says,

> He humbled you, causing you to hunger and then feeding you with manna, which neither you nor your fathers had known, to teach you that man does not live on bread alone but on every word that comes from the mouth of the LORD.

God taught the nation through His divine providence— through putting them in a situation where they could not simply go to the cupboard for their daily bread—that they were utterly dependent upon Him. God was leading the nation into a land where material provision would be "naturally" plentiful (see Deuteronomy 8:7-9). He knew they would be tempted by the pride of their own hearts to say, "My power and the strength of my hands have produced this wealth for me" (verse 17). So before they entered the land, God taught them of their dependence through His divine providence.

God's Wisdom in World Affairs

Going beyond our own personal circumstances, we can also say that God's infinite wisdom, directing His sovereign power, governs the world. As we look around us it does seem that much of the world is outside of God's control and that much of what happens makes no sense. Why should 109 children suffocate under a mud slide in South Wales, or thousands die in Rwanda or Darfur? Why do seemingly more "wicked" rulers so frequently prosper in the arena of world affairs? Why do the rich get richer and the poor get poorer? Granted we live in a sin-cursed world, and all these things could simply be attributed to the sinfulness of mankind.

But if we accept that God is sovereign, as we saw in earlier chapters, then we must conclude that God is in control of even these terrible circumstances and is guiding them with His infinite wisdom to their appointed purpose. They are not just an assortment of uncontrolled and unrelated events. Rather, they are all part of God's perfect pattern and plan, which will one day be shown to be for both His glory and the good of His Church. Professor Berkouwer is again helpful when he writes,

> All facets of life are embraced in God's rule. The plurality of life is brought under one perspective. It is not that there is a confusion of countless atomistic events in all of which God's activity is manifest. There is a pivot, a centrum which unifies the diversity of His activity. The unity includes progress of events from His promise at the time of the fall to the completion of the formation of His holy people.[8]

Just as we should learn to stop asking why, or searching for rational explanations, or seeking to discover what "good" there is in our own adversities, so we must also learn to quiet our hearts in regard to God's government of the universe. We must come to the place where we can say, in the words of David, "I have stilled and quieted my soul" (Psalm 131:2) about all the tragedies that come on mankind around the world.

The Puritan John Flavel wrote,

Believe firmly that the management of all the affairs of
this world, whether public or personal, is in the hands
of your all-wise God. . . . Resign up yourselves to the
wisdom of God, and lean not to your own understanding. . . . do not thou presume to be the governor of the
world, but leave the reins of government in his hands
that made it, and best knows how to rule it.[9]

This does not mean we are to become indifferent and callous
to the tremendous amount of suffering that goes on around the
world. We should pray for the victims of tragedies and, where
opportunity permits, respond tangibly to the relief of their sufferings. But we can be compassionate without questioning God
about His government of the world. An unreserved trust of God,
when we don't understand what is happening or why, is the only
road to peace and comfort and joy. God wants us to honor Him
by trusting Him, but He also desires that we experience the
peace and joy that come as a result.

Discussion Questions

1. What is wisdom?
2. How does God show that He has perfect wisdom?
3. The good for which God works in our lives is not necessarily comfort or happiness but Christlikeness in ever
   increasing measure.
   a. Think of some specific situations. What is the
      good you are aiming at in each situation?
   b. In each situation, how is your agenda the same
      as or different from God's?

4. Why can't we build godly character without suffering?

5. Read Isaiah 55:8-9. What situation(s) come to mind when you think of God's ways being different from your ways?

6. Does this chapter help you trust God in the situations where you don't know why He has allowed something? If so, how? If not, what's missing for you?

EXPERIENCING GOD'S LOVE

Who shall separate us from the love of Christ?
Shall trouble or hardship or persecution or famine
or nakedness or danger or sword? . . .
No, in all these things we are more than
conquerors through him who loved us.

ROMANS 8:35,37

A friend of mine who spends a good amount of time encouraging others found himself distraught over the spiritual struggles of one of his children. In desperation he cried out, "God, I think I'm doing a better job taking care of Your children than You are of mine." He told me, "As soon as I said it, I repented to the Lord." Nevertheless, his frustrating experience illustrates a point. Most of us are tempted, from time to time, to question God's love for us.

I can identify with my friend. Once when one of our children was going through a series of difficult experiences, I said, "God, I wouldn't treat my child the way You are treating her."

I, too, had to repent of my brash words and work through the assurance in the Scriptures that God's love is just as real in times of adversity as it is in times of blessing.

It seems the more we come to believe in and accept the sovereignty of God over every event of our lives, the more we are tempted to question His love. We think, "If God is in control of this adversity and can do something about it, why doesn't He?" Rabbi Kushner chose to believe in a God who is good but not sovereign. Sometimes we are tempted, if only momentarily, to believe in a sovereign God who is not good. Satan, whose very first act toward man was to question the goodness of God, will even plant the thought in our minds that God is up in heaven mocking us in our distress.

But we are not forced to choose between the sovereignty and the goodness of God. The Bible affirms both His sovereignty and His goodness with equal emphasis. References to His goodness and lovingkindness, like His sovereignty, appear on almost every page of Scripture.

The apostle John said, "God is love" (1 John 4:8). This succinct statement, along with its parallel one, "God is light" (1 John 1:5, that is, God is holy), sums up the essential character of God, as revealed to us in the Scriptures. Just as it is impossible in the very nature of God for Him to be anything but perfectly holy, so it is impossible for Him to be anything but perfectly good.[1]

Because God is love, it is an essential part of His nature to do good and show mercy to His creatures. Psalm 145 speaks of His "abundant goodness," of His being "rich in love" and "good to all," of having "compassion on all he has made," and of being "loving toward all he has made" (verses 7-9,17). Even in His role of Judge of rebellious men, He declares, "I take no pleasure in the death of the wicked" (Ezekiel 33:11).

When we are in the midst of adversity and, as it frequently seems to happen, calamity after calamity seems to be surging in upon us, we will be tempted to doubt God's love. Not only do we struggle with our own doubts, but Satan seizes these occasions to whisper accusations against God, such as, "If He loved you, He wouldn't have allowed this to happen." My own experience suggests that Satan attacks us far more in the area of God's love than either His sovereignty or His wisdom.

Even righteous Job, who at the beginning of his calamities was able to say, "The LORD gave and the LORD has taken away; may the name of the LORD be praised" (Job 1:21), finally came to the place where he too questioned the goodness of God. He said, "God denies me justice," and "It profits a man nothing when he tries to please God" (Job 34:5,9).

If God is perfect in His love and abundant in His goodness, how do we take a stand against our own doubts and the temptations of Satan to question the goodness of God? What truths about God do we need to store up in our hearts to use as weapons against temptations to doubt His love?

God's Love at Calvary

There is no doubt that the most convincing evidence of God's love in all of Scripture is His giving His Son to die for our sins.

> This is how God showed his love among us: He sent
> his one and only Son into the world that we might live
> through him. This is love: not that we loved God, but

that he loved us and sent his Son as an atoning sacrifice for our sins. (1 John 4:9-10)

John said that God is love, and this is how He showed His
love, by sending His Son to die for us. Our greatest need is not
freedom from adversity. All the possible calamities that could
occur in this life cannot in any way be compared with the
absolute calamity of eternal separation from God. Jesus said no
earthly joy could compare with the eternal joy of our names
written in heaven (see Luke 10:20). In like manner, no earthly
adversity can compare with that awful calamity of God's eternal
judgment in hell.

So when John said that God showed His love by sending His
Son, he was saying God showed His love by meeting our greatest need—a need so great that no other need can even come
close to it in comparison. If we want proof of God's love for us,
then we must look first at the Cross where God offered up His
Son as a sacrifice for our sins. Calvary is the one objective,
absolute, irrefutable proof of God's love for us.

The extent of God's love at Calvary is seen in both the infinite cost to Him of giving His one and only Son, and in the
rebellion and profound lostness of those He loved. God could
not remove our sins without an infinite cost to both Himself and
His Son. And because of their great love for us, both were willing—yes, more than merely willing—to pay that great cost, the
Father in giving His one and only Son, and the Son in laying
down His life for us. One of the essential characteristics of love
is the element of self-sacrifice, and this was demonstrated for us
to its ultimate in God's love at Calvary.

Consider also the miserable and wretched condition of those

God loved. Paul said, "But God demonstrates his own love for us in this: While we were still sinners, Christ died for us" (Romans 5:8). It is sometimes difficult for those of us who grew up in morally upright or Christian homes to appreciate the force of Paul's statement, "while we were still sinners." Because many of us were generally upright and morally decent people in the eyes of society and in our own eyes, it is difficult for us to see ourselves as God saw us—as enemies of God, completely alienated from Him (Colossians 1:21).

In Ephesians 2, Paul says we followed the ways of this world (verse 2), that is, of the ungodly society around us. Not only did we follow the ways of the ungodly society, we even followed the Devil, whom Paul calls the ruler of the kingdom of the air. Perhaps it was not by a conscious deliberate choice that we followed the Devil, but we did so because we were under his power and dominion (see Acts 26:18; Colossians 1:13). We were actually servants of the archenemy of God. Further, Paul says that we spent our days gratifying the cravings of our sinful nature, following its desires and thoughts (verse 3). We lived for ourselves, our ambitions, our desires, our pleasures. And then, as Paul continues this description of us in our unsaved state, he concludes with the statement that we were by nature objects of God's wrath. It is while we were in this state of total alienation from God that Christ died for us.

Whenever we are tempted to doubt God's love for us, we should go back to the Cross. We should reason somewhat in this fashion: If God loved me enough to give His Son to die for me when I was His enemy, surely He loves me enough to care for me now that I am His child. Having loved me to the ultimate extent at the Cross, He cannot possibly fail to love me in my times of adversity. Having given such a priceless gift as His Son, surely He will also give all else that is consistent with His glory and my good.

It may seem cold and even unspiritual to seek to "reason" through the truths of God's love in times of heartache, pain, and disappointment. But Paul gave us a helpful model for this form of reasoning—an argument from the greater to the lesser—when he said, "He who did not spare his own Son, but gave him up for us all—how will he not also, along with him, graciously give us all things?" (Romans 8:32). Paul reasoned that if God loved us so much to give us the greatest conceivable gift, then surely He will not withhold any lesser blessing from us.

God's Family Love

By God's grace having trusted Christ as our Savior, we who are believers have been brought into the very family of God. He has covenanted with us to be our God and we to be His people (see Hebrews 8:10). Through Christ He has adopted us as His children and has sent His Holy Spirit to live within us and to testify with our spirit that we are His children. The Holy Spirit bears witness within us to this filial relationship we have with God when He causes us to cry in our hearts, "*Abba*, Father" (Romans 8:15-16). Paul's use of that word is intended to convey to us how deeply the Spirit assures us that we are indeed children of the Most High God, now our heavenly Father.

As our heavenly Father, God loves us, His children, with a very special love, a fatherly love. He calls us His "chosen people, holy and *dearly loved*" (Colossians 3:12, emphasis added). As incredible as it may seem, "He will take great delight in you . . .

will rejoice over you with singing" (Zephaniah 3:17). He delights in us as a father delights in his children. As Matthew Henry observed when commenting on Zephaniah 3:17, "The great God not only loves his saints, but he loves to love them."

In Psalm 103:11, David speaks of God's fatherly love in this way: "For as high as the heavens are above the earth, so great is his love for those who fear him." In the last chapter, we saw that God's *ways* are higher than our ways, as the heavens are higher than the earth. Here we see that God's *love* for His own is as high as the heavens are above the earth. Just as God's wisdom, like the height of the heavens, cannot be measured, so God's love for us cannot be measured. No calamity that may come upon us, however great it may be, can carry us beyond the pale of God's fatherly love for us.

God's Love in Christ

This infinite, measureless love of God is poured out upon us, not because of who we are or what we are, but because we are united with Christ. In Romans 8:39, Paul says that "[nothing] will be able to separate us from the love of God that is in Christ Jesus our Lord." The love of God flows to us entirely through, or in, Jesus Christ. The term *in Christ* is one Paul uses frequently to refer to our spiritually organic union with Jesus Christ. Jesus speaks of this same union in His metaphor of the vine and its branches in John 15. Just as the branches are organically related to the vine in a life-giving union, so believers, in a spiritual sense, are organically united to Christ.

It is important to grasp this crucial concept that God's love to us is *in Christ*. Just as God's love to His *Son* cannot change, so

His love to us cannot change, because we are in union with the One He loves. God's love to us can no more waver than His love to His Son can waver.

We are constantly tempted to look within ourselves to seek to find some reason why God should love us. Such searching is, of course, usually discouraging. We usually find within ourselves reasons we think God should *not* love us. Such searching is also unbiblical. The Bible is quite clear that God does not look within us for a reason to love us. He loves us because we are in Christ Jesus. When He looks at us, He does not see us resplendent in our own good works, even good works as Christians. Rather, He sees us united to His beloved Son, clothed in Christ's righteousness.

God's Sovereign Love

In earlier chapters we looked at the sovereignty of God over all of His universe. That sovereignty is exercised primarily for His glory. But because you and I are in Christ Jesus, *His* glory and *our* good are linked together. Because we are united with Christ, whatever is for His glory is also for our good. And whatever is for our good is for His glory.

Therefore, we can, with scriptural warrant, say that God exercises His sovereignty on our behalf. Paul says in Ephesians 1:22-23, "God placed all things under his feet and appointed him [Christ] to be head over everything for the church, which is his body, the fullness of him who fills everything in every way." That is, Christ reigns over the entire universe for the benefit of His body, the Church.

The union of God's sovereignty and His love for the benefit

of His people is expressed in another symbol—the shepherd and his sheep—in Isaiah 40. In verses 10-11, the prophet says,

> See, the Sovereign LORD comes with power,
> and his arm rules for him. . . .
> He tends his flock like a shepherd:
> He gathers the lambs in his arms
> and carries them close to his heart;
> he gently leads those that have young.

No more picturesque symbol of God's love for us can be given than that of the faithful and tender Shepherd carrying His lambs close to His heart. And we are carried in the arms of sovereign power.

The Assurance of God's Love

So often we do not *see* or *sense* God's sovereign love exercised on our behalf. Instead, we see ourselves beset with all kinds of calamities that come rolling in upon us. We see ourselves as the victims of "nature's cruel fate," of the injustices of other people, and of adversities that occur with no rational cause.

It is at times like this that we must take our stand by faith on the assurances of God's love given to us in the Scriptures. We cannot evade one of the basic principles of the Christian life, "We live by faith, not by sight" (2 Corinthians 5:7). Certainly our faith frequently wavers and, just as we may momentarily question the wisdom of God, we will momentarily question the goodness and love of God. We will be like David when he said, "In my alarm I said, 'I am cut off from your sight!'" (Psalm

31:22). That is often our initial reaction when adversity strikes us. We feel cut off from God's face, from His love and tender care.

But we must also learn to say with David, "Yet you heard my cry for mercy when I called to you for help" (Psalm 31:22). God cannot forsake us because we are His children, in blessed union with His Son. We cannot be cut off from His sight. But we can be cut off from the *assurance* of His love when we allow doubt and unbelief to gain a foothold in our hearts.

Anyone who has ever felt cut off from the Lord's face and forsaken by Him can ponder with great feeling the misery of the nation of Judah following her destruction by the Babylonian army. The writer of Lamentations (traditionally accepted to be Jeremiah) muses: "I remember my affliction and my wandering, the bitterness and the gall. I well remember them, and my soul is downcast within me" (Lamentations 3:19-20).

The writer has reached the bottom of the barrel emotionally and spiritually. But then the mood changes completely, as the writer says in verse 21, "Yet this I call to mind and therefore I have hope." There follows one of the greatest passages in all of the Bible—a passage that has brought hope and encouragement to countless believers down through the centuries: "Because of the LORD's great love we are not consumed, for his compassions never fail. They are new every morning; great is your faithfulness" (Lamentations 3:22-23).

What was it that caused such a dramatic mood change in the heart of the writer? He turns from the circumstances at hand to the Lord. He was not cut off from God. Even the nation in the depth of its sin was not cut off from God's love. God disciplined the nation severely, but He did not cease to love it. We, too, if we would speak of the Lord's great faithfulness, must turn from our circumstances to the Lord. We must see our circumstances through God's love instead of, as we are prone to do, seeing God's love through our circumstances.

God's Unfailing Love

A very frequent expression in the Psalms is God's *unfailing love*. For example, Psalm 32:10 says, "The LORD's unfailing love surrounds the man who trusts in him." Think of what that means. *God's love cannot fail.* It is steadfast, constant, and fixed. In all the adversities we go through, God's love is unfailing. As He says to us in Isaiah 54:10, " 'Though the mountains be shaken and the hills be removed, yet my unfailing love for you will not be shaken nor my covenant of peace be removed,' says the LORD, who has compassion on you." And because His love cannot fail, He will allow into our lives only the pain and heartache that is for our ultimate good.

Even the grief that He Himself brings into our lives is tempered with His compassion. "Though he brings grief, he will show compassion, so great is his unfailing love" (Lamentations 3:32). The assurance here is that God will *show* compassion. It is not enough to say that He *is* compassionate, but He will *show* compassion. That is, even the fires of affliction will be tempered by His compassion, which arises out of His unfailing love. *Our afflictions are always accompanied with the compassion and consolation of God.*

Paul experienced God's compassion in the midst of his grief. To prevent pride in his life, God gave him a thorn in his flesh. What the thorn was we do not know, but we know it was a severe affliction for Paul. On three occasions he pleaded with the Lord to take it away, but God said no. Instead, God said, "My grace is sufficient for you" (2 Corinthians 12:9). God brought grief into Paul's life for his good, but he also showed compassion. He gave grace, in this case divine strength, to bear the grief. He did not leave Paul to bear the thorn in his flesh alone. So eventually Paul came to rejoice in his affliction, because through it he experienced God's overcoming power.

God does not give us all the divine strength we need for the Christian life the day we trust Christ. Rather, David speaks of God's goodness, which is stored up for those who fear Him (see Psalm 31:19). Just as we are to store up (the meaning of "hidden" in Psalm 119:11) God's Word in our hearts against a time of temptation, so God stores up goodness or grace for our times of adversity. We do not receive it before we need it, but we never receive it too late.

I think of a physician whose son was born with an incurable birth defect, leaving him crippled for life. I asked the father how he felt when he, who had dedicated his life to treating the illnesses of other people, was confronted with an incurable condition in his own son. He told me his biggest problem was the tendency to capsule the next twenty years of his son's life into that initial moment when he learned of his son's condition. Viewed that way, the adversity was overwhelming. God does not give twenty years of grace today. Rather, He gives it day by day.

God's Presence with Us

God's love is unfailing; His grace is always sufficient. But there is even more good news. He is *with us* in our troubles. He does not merely send grace from heaven to meet our trials. He Himself comes to help us. He says to us, "Do not be afraid . . . for I myself will help you" (Isaiah 41:14).

In Isaiah 43:2, God says,

> "When you pass through the waters, I will be with you; and when you pass through the rivers, they will not sweep over you. When you walk through the fire, you will not be burned; the flames will not set you ablaze."

God promises specifically to be *with us* in our sorrows and afflictions. He will not spare us from the waters of sorrow and the fires of adversity, but He will go through them with us. Even when the waters and the fires are those that God Himself brings into our lives, He still goes through them with us. Most of the gracious promises of God to be with us were given first to the nation of Judah during times of national spiritual decline. God, through His prophets, continually warned the people of coming judgment; yet in the midst of those warnings, we find these incredible promises of His being with them. God judged His people, but He did not forsake them. Even in their judgments, He was with them. As Isaiah said, "In all their distress he too was distressed" (Isaiah 63:9).

So regardless of the nature or the cause of our adversities, God goes through them with us. He says, "I will strengthen you and help you; I will uphold you with my righteous right hand" (Isaiah 41:10). It is often in the very midst of our adversities that we experience the most delightful manifestations of His love. As Paul said in 2 Corinthians 1:5, "For just as the sufferings of Christ flow over into our lives, so also through Christ our comfort overflows."

Because we are in union with Christ, He shares our adversities. Nothing can separate us from His love. In the words of Paul, "Neither height nor depth, nor anything else in all creation, will be able to separate us from the love of God that is in Christ Jesus our Lord" (Romans 8:39). God's unfailing love for us is an objective fact affirmed over and over in the Scriptures. It is true whether we believe it or not. Our doubts do not destroy God's love, nor does our faith create it. It originates in the very nature of God, who is love, and it flows to us through our union with His beloved Son.

Discussion Questions

1. Why is the Cross the ultimate expression of God's love for us? You might look at Romans 5:6-8 and 1 John 4:9-10.
2. Read Mark 15:16-39 slowly and meditatively. Where, if at all, do you see God's love for you in this event?
3. If the Cross doesn't grip you as evidence of God's love for you, why do you suppose that's the case? What can you do about that?
4. What experiences in your life have tempted you to doubt God's love?
5. When you have doubted God's love, what (if anything) has helped you regain confidence in His love?
6. Why doesn't God do whatever He can to make us happy and free from pain? After all, as human parents we want that for our children.
7. Read Lamentations 3:17-24. What can you learn from Jeremiah about handling feelings of disappointment and defeat?

GROWING THROUGH ADVERSITY

Consider it pure joy, my brothers, whenever you face
trials of many kinds, because you know that the
testing of your faith develops perseverance.
Perseverance must finish its work so that you may
be mature and complete, not lacking anything.
JAMES 1:2-4

One of the many fascinating events in nature is the emergence of the cecropia moth from its cocoon—an event that occurs only with much struggle on the part of the moth to free itself. The story is frequently told of someone who watched a moth go through this struggle. In an effort to help—and not realizing the necessity of the struggle—the viewer snipped the shell of the cocoon. Soon the moth came out with its wings all crimped and shriveled. But as the person watched, the wings remained weak. The moth, which in a few moments would have stretched those wings to fly, was now doomed to crawling out its brief life in frustration of ever being the beautiful creature God created it to be.

What the person in the story did not realize was that the struggle to emerge from the cocoon was an essential part of developing the muscle system of the moth's body and pushing the body fluids out into the wings to expand them. By unwisely seeking to cut short the moth's struggle, the watcher had actually crippled the moth and doomed its existence.

The adversities of life are much like the cocoon of the cecropia moth. God uses them to develop the spiritual "muscle system" of our lives. As James says in our text for this chapter, "The testing of your faith [through trials of many kinds] develops perseverance," and perseverance leads to maturity of our character.

We can be sure that the development of a beautiful Christlike character will not occur in our lives without adversity. Think of those lovely graces that Paul calls the fruit of the Spirit in Galatians 5:22-23. The first four traits he mentions—love, joy, peace, and patience—can only be developed in the womb of adversity.

We may think we have true Christian love until someone offends us or treats us unjustly. Then we begin to see anger and resentment well up within us. We may conclude we have learned about genuine Christian joy until our lives are shattered by an unexpected calamity or grievous disappointment. Adversities spoil our peace and sorely try our patience. God uses those difficulties to reveal to us our need to grow, so that we will reach out to Him to change us more and more into the likeness of His Son.

However, we shrink from adversity and, to use the terms from the moth illustration, we want God to snip the cocoon of adversity we often find ourselves in and release us. But just as God has more wisdom and love for the moth than its viewer did, so He has more wisdom and love for us than we do for ourselves. He will not remove the adversity until we have profited from it and developed in whatever way He intended in bringing or allowing it into our lives.

Both Paul and James speak of rejoicing in our sufferings (see Romans 5:3-4; James 1:2-4). Most of us, if we are honest with ourselves, have difficulty with that idea. Endure them, perhaps, but rejoice? That often seems like an unreasonable expectation. We are not masochistic; we don't enjoy pain.

But Paul and James both say that we should rejoice in our trials because of their beneficial results. It is not the adversity considered in itself that is to be the ground of our joy. Rather, it is the expectation of the results, the development of our character, that should cause us to rejoice in adversity. God does not ask us to rejoice because we have lost our job, or a loved one has been stricken with cancer, or a child has been born with an incurable birth defect. But He does tell us to rejoice because we believe He is in control of those circumstances and is at work through them for our ultimate good.

The Christian life is intended to be one of continuous growth. We all want to grow, but we often resist the process. This is because we tend to focus on the events of adversity themselves, rather than looking with the eye of faith beyond the events to what God is doing in our lives. It was said of Jesus that He "for the joy set before him endured the cross, scorning its shame" (Hebrews 12:2). Christ's death on the cross with its intense physical agony and infinite spiritual suffering of bearing God's wrath for our sins was the greatest calamity to ever come upon a human being. Yet Jesus could look beyond that suffering to the joy set before Him. And, as the writer of Hebrews said, we are to fix our eyes on Him and follow His example. We are to look beyond our adversity to what God is doing in our lives and rejoice in the certainty that He is at work in us to cause us to grow.

We Learn from Adversity

There are several things we can do to learn from adversity and receive the benefits that God intends. First, we can *submit* to it—not reluctantly as the defeated general submits to his conqueror, but voluntarily as the patient on the operating table submits to the skilled hand of the surgeon as he wields his knife. Do not try to frustrate the gracious purpose of God by resisting His providence in your life. Rather, insofar as you are able to see what God is doing, make His purpose your purpose.

This does not mean we should not use all legitimate means at our disposal to minimize the effects of adversity. It means we should accept from God's hand the success or failure of those means as He wills, and at all times seek to learn whatever He might be teaching us.

Sometimes we will perceive quite clearly what God is doing, and in those instances we should respond to God's teaching in humble obedience. At other times we may not be able to see at all what He is doing in our lives. At those times, we should respond in humble faith, trusting Him to work out in our lives that which we need to learn. Both attitudes are important, and God wants one at one time and the other at another time.

Second, to profit most from adversity, we should *bring the Word of God to bear upon the situation.* As we seek to relate the Scriptures to our adversities, we'll find we will not only profit from the circumstances themselves, but we will gain new insight

GROWING THROUGH ADVERSITY   113

into the Scriptures. Martin Luther reportedly said, "Were it not for tribulation I should not understand the Scriptures." Although we may be going to the Scriptures to learn how to respond to our adversities, we find those adversities in turn help us to understand the Scriptures. It is not that we will learn from adversity something different from what we can learn from the Scriptures. Rather, adversity enhances the teaching of God's Word and makes it more profitable to us. In some instances it clarifies our understanding or causes us to see truths we had passed over before. At other times it will transform "head knowledge" into "heart knowledge" as theological theory becomes a reality to us.

The Puritan Daniel Dyke said,

The word, then, is the storehouse of all instruction.
Look not for any new diverse doctrine to be taught
thee by affliction, which is not in the word. For, in truth,
herein stands our teaching by affliction, that it fits and
prepares us for the word, by breaking and sub-dividing
the stubbornness of our hearts, and making them pli-
able, and capable of the impression of the word.[1]

Third, in order to profit from our adversities we must *remember* them and the lessons we learned from them. God wants us to do more than simply endure our trials, even more than merely find comfort in them. He wants us to remember them, not just as trials or sorrows, but as His disciplines—His means of bringing about growth in our lives. He said to the Israelites, "Remember how the LORD your God led you all the way in the desert these forty years, to humble you and to test

you. . . . He humbled you, causing you to hunger and then feeding you with manna . . . to teach you that man does not live on
bread alone but on every word that comes from the mouth of
the LORD" (Deuteronomy 8:2-3).

The "word that comes from the mouth of the LORD" in this
passage is not the Word of Scripture but the word of God's providence (see Psalms 33:6,9 and 148:5 for similar usage). God
wanted to teach the Israelites that they were dependent upon
Him for their daily bread. He did this—not by incorporating
this truth into the law of Moses—but by bringing adversity in
the form of hunger into their lives. But in order to profit from
this lesson they must *remember* it.[2]

Pruning

Jesus said that "every branch that does bear fruit [God] prunes
so that it will be even more fruitful" (John 15:2). In the natural
realm, pruning is important for fruit bearing. An unpruned vine
will produce a great deal of unproductive growth but little fruit.
Cutting away unwanted and useless growth forces the plant to
use its life to produce fruit.

In the spiritual realm, God must prune us. Because, even as
believers we still have a sinful nature, we tend to pour our spiritual energies into that which is not true fruit. We tend to seek
position, success, and reputation even in the Body of Christ. We
tend to depend upon natural talents and human wisdom.

God uses adversity to loosen our grip on those things that
are not true fruit. A severe illness or the death of someone dear
to us, the loss of material substance or the tarnishing of our
reputation, the turning aside of friends or the dashing of our

cherished dreams on the rocks of failure, cause us to think about what is really important in life. Position or possessions or even reputation no longer seem so important. We begin to relinquish our desires and expectations—even good ones—to the sovereign will of God. We come more and more to depend on God and to desire only that which will count for eternity. God is pruning us so that we will be more fruitful.

Holiness

Who of us does not read that list of Christian virtues called the fruit of the Spirit—love, joy, peace, patience, kindness, goodness, faithfulness, gentleness, and self-control (Galatians 5:22-23)—and agree we want all those traits in our lives? We even begin to think we are making good progress in growing in them.

But then adversity comes. We find we are unable to love, from the depths of our hearts, the person who is the instrument of the adversity. We find we don't want to forgive that person. We realize we are not disposed to trust God. Unbelief and resentment surge within us. We are dismayed with ourselves. The growth in Christian character we thought had occurred in our lives seems to vanish like a vapor. We feel as if we are back in spiritual kindergarten again. But through this experience God has revealed to us some of the remaining corruption within us.

Jesus said, "Blessed are the poor in spirit. . . . Blessed are those who mourn. . . . Blessed are those who hunger and thirst for righteousness" (Matthew 5:3-4,6). All of these descriptions refer to the believer who has been humbled over his sinfulness, who mourns because of it, and yearns with all his heart for God to change him. But no one adopts this attitude without being exposed to the evil and corruption of his own heart. God uses adversity to do this.

The Scriptures say: "God disciplines us [through adversity] for our good, that we may share in his holiness" (Hebrews 12:10). In making us holy, God goes deeper than just specific sins we may be conscious of. He wants to get at the root cause: the corruption of our sinful nature manifested in the rebellion of our wills, the perversity of our affections, and the spiritual ignorance of our minds. God uses adversity to enlighten our minds about our own needs as well as the teachings of Scripture. He uses adversity to reign in our affections that have been drawn out to unholy desires and to subdue our stubborn and rebellious wills. As we look to God to use His discipline in our lives, we may be sure it will in due time produce "a harvest of righteousness and peace for those who have been trained by it" (Hebrews 12:11).

Dependence

Jesus said, "Apart from me you can do nothing" (John 15:5). Apart from our union with Christ and a total reliance upon Him we can do nothing that glorifies God. Yet we live in a world that worships independence and self-reliance.

God has to teach us through adversity to rely on Him instead of ourselves. Even the apostle Paul said of his difficulties, which he described as "far beyond our ability to endure," that they occurred so "that we might not rely on ourselves but on God, who raises the dead" (2 Corinthians 1:8-9). God allowed Paul and his band of men to be brought into a situation so desperate that they despaired even of life itself. They had no place to turn except to God.

Paul had to learn dependence on God in the spiritual as well as the physical realm. Whatever his thorn in the flesh was (see 2 Corinthians 12:7-10), it was an adversity that Paul desperately wanted to be rid of. But God let it remain, not only to curb any tendency for pride in Paul's heart, but also to teach him to rely on God's strength. Paul had to learn that it was not his strength but God's grace—God's enabling power—that he must depend on.

I am a person of many weaknesses and few natural strengths. My physical limitations, though not apparent to most people, prevent my relating to other men through golf, tennis, or other recreational sports. I feel this keenly, and for some years I struggled frequently with God about it. But I have at last concluded that my weaknesses are actually channels for *His* strength. After many years, I think I am finally at the point where I can say with Paul, "I delight in weaknesses. . . . For when I am weak, then I am strong" (2 Corinthians 12:10).

It does not matter whether you are predominantly a person of strengths or weaknesses on the natural level. You may be the most competent person in your field, but you can be sure that if God is going to use you He will cause you to feel keenly your dependence on Him. He will often blight the very thing we feel confident in, so that we will learn to depend on Him, not on ourselves.

Perseverance

To the recipients of the letter to the Hebrews, who were experiencing persecution and hardship for their faith in Christ, the writer wrote, "You need to persevere so that when you have done the will of God, you will receive what he has promised" (Hebrews 10:36). And, "Let us run with perseverance the race marked out for us" (12:1).

Perseverance is the quality of character that enables one to pursue a goal in spite of obstacles and difficulties. God calls us to do more than simply bear the load of adversity. He calls us to persevere (to press forward) in the face of it. Note how the writer of Hebrews focuses on reaching the goal: "When you have *done* the will of God" and "*run* . . . the race marked out for us." The Christian life is meant to be active, not passive. The Christian is called to pursue with perseverance the will of God.

Each of us has been given a race to run, a will of God to do. All of us encounter innumerable obstacles and occasions for discouragement. To run the race and finish well we must develop perseverance. How can we do it?

Both Paul and James give us the same answer. Paul said, "We know that suffering produces perseverance," and James said, "The testing of your faith develops perseverance" (Romans 5:3; James 1:3). We see here a mutually enhancing effect. Adversity produces perseverance, and perseverance enables us to meet adversity.

Though perseverance is developed in the crucible of adversity, it is energized by faith. It is God's strength, not ours, that enables us to persevere. But we lay hold of His strength through faith. Jesus said, "Apart from me you can do nothing," and Paul said, "I can do everything through him who gives me strength" (John 15:5; Philippians 4:13). Jesus and Paul state two sides of the same truth: Without His strength we can do nothing, but with it we can do all we need to do.

Service

God also brings adversity into our lives to equip us for more effective service. All that we have considered so far—pruning, holiness, dependence, and perseverance—contribute to making us useful instruments in God's service.

The apostle Paul wrote that "[God] comforts us in all our troubles, so that we can comfort those in any trouble with the comfort we ourselves have received from God" (2 Corinthians 1:4). Everyone faces times of adversity, and everyone needs a compassionate and caring friend to come alongside to comfort and encourage during those times. As we experience God's comfort and encouragement in our adversities, we are equipped to be His instrument of comfort and encouragement to others. To the extent we are able to lay hold of the great truths of the sovereignty, wisdom, and love of God and find comfort and encouragement from them in our adversities, we will be able to minister to others in their times of distress. We can encourage another person best by pointing to the trustworthiness of God as it is revealed to us in Scripture.

The Fellowship of Suffering

The apostle John, writing to the persecuted believers of the seven churches in Asia, identified himself as "your brother and companion in the suffering . . . that [is] ours in Jesus" (Revelation 1:9). The Greek word that is translated as *companion* means a "fellow sharer." It is a form of the word *koinonia* from which we get our word *fellowship*.

So, John introduces us to yet another way in which we profit from adversity: the privilege of entering into a special fellowship with other believers who are also in the throes of adversity. Trials and afflictions have a leveling effect among believers. It has often been said that "the ground is level at the foot of the cross." That is, regardless of our wealth, or power, or station in life, we are all alike in our need for a Savior. In the same way, we are all alike subject to adversity. It strikes the rich and the poor, the powerful and the weak, the superior and the subordinate, all without distinction.

Trials and afflictions tend to break down barriers between people and dissolve any appearance of self-sufficiency we may have. We find our hearts warmed and drawn toward one another. We sometimes worship together with another person, pray together, and even serve together in the ministry without ever truly feeling a bond of fellowship. But then, in a strange way, adversity strikes us both. Immediately we sense a new bond of fellowship in Christ, the fellowship of suffering.

Relationship with God

Perhaps the most valuable way we profit from adversity is in the deepening of our relationship with God. Through adversity we learn to bow before His sovereignty, to trust His wisdom, and to experience the consolations of His love, until we come to the place where we can say with Job, "My ears had heard of you but now my eyes have seen you" (Job 42:5). We begin to pass from knowing *about* God to knowing God Himself in a personal and intimate way.

We have just considered the fellowship of suffering among believers. In Philippians 3:10, Paul speaks of the fellowship of sharing in the sufferings of Jesus Christ, that is, of believers sharing with our Lord in His sufferings. The passage reads as follows:

> I want to know Christ and the power of his resurrec-
> tion and the fellowship of sharing in his sufferings,
> becoming like him in his death.

This verse has given expression to the deepest heart cry of believers down through the centuries: the desire to know Christ in an ever-increasing intimate, personal way. If we are to experience the power of His resurrection, we can also be sure we will experience the fellowship of His sufferings.

It will help us to appreciate the truth that Paul is teaching in Philippians 3:10, if we understand that the suffering Paul envisions is not limited to persecution for the sake of the gospel. It includes all adversity that overtakes the believer and that has as its ultimate purpose his conformity to Christ, described here by Paul as "becoming like him in his death."

Repeatedly in the Bible, we see men and women of God drawn into a deeper relationship with God through adversity. There is no doubt that all the circumstances in the long delay of the birth of Isaac and then the experience of taking his only son up to the mountain to offer as a sacrifice brought Abraham into a much deeper relationship with God. The psalms are replete with expressions of ever-deepening knowledge of God as the psalmists seek Him in times of adversity (see, for example, Psalms 23; 42; 61; and 62).

For the believer, all pain has meaning; all adversity is profitable. To us it often appears completely senseless and irrational, but to God none of it is either senseless or irrational. He has a purpose in every pain He brings or allows in our lives. We can be sure that in some way He intends it for our profit and His glory.

Discussion Questions

1. Consider Galatians 5:22-23. How does adversity help us develop the following?

love

joy

peace

patience (the ability to endure suffering for long
periods without giving up or losing one's temper)

gentleness (a firm but forgiving response to wrong-
doers)

self-control

2. How does adversity help us grow in these areas?

pruning—loosening our grip on desires and expectations, even good ones, so that we can embrace
God's will

holiness—exposing our rebelliousness and wrong
desires

dependence—relying on God instead of ourselves

perseverance—pursuing a goal despite obstacles

service—being God's means to comfort and encourage others' fellowship of suffering—uniting our
hearts with other believers' intimacy with Christ—
sharing in His sufferings

3. How has God used adversity to help you grow?

4. How can Romans 5:1-5 (or some other passage that
comes to mind, perhaps from this chapter) help you
grow through adversity rather than crumbling under it?

5. If you are experiencing adversity right now, what do
you think are some fruitful ways of responding to it?

CHOOSING TO TRUST GOD

When I am afraid,
I will trust in you.
In God, whose Word I praise,
in God I trust; I will not be afraid.
What can mortal man do to me?

PSALM 56:3-4

A number of years ago, my first wife, who is now with the Lord, was found to have a large malignant tumor in the abdominal cavity. After eight weeks of radiation therapy and another month of waiting, the doctor ordered a CAT scan to determine if the tumor had been successfully resolved. The day before she was to learn the results of the CAT scan, my wife found herself quite apprehensive and anxious over the news she would hear the next day.

For some days she had been turning to Psalm 42:11 for assurance during this difficult time. The verse says, "Why are you downcast, O my soul? Why so disturbed within me? Put your hope in God, for I will yet praise him, my Savior and my God."

Turning to Psalm 42:11 that day, she said, "Lord, I choose not to be downcast, I choose not to be disturbed, I choose to put my hope in You." She told me later, as she recounted this to me, that her feelings did not change immediately, but after a while they did. Her heart was calmed as she deliberately chose to trust God.

David, in his times of distress, also chose to trust God. In Psalm 56:3-4, our text for this chapter, David admitted he was afraid. David was not cocky or arrogant. Despite the fact that he was a warrior of great skill and courage, there were times when he was afraid. The heading of Psalm 56 indicates the occasion of David's writing: "When the Philistines had seized him in Gath." The historical narrative of that incident says that he "was very much afraid of Achish king of Gath" (1 Samuel 21:12).

But despite David's fear, he said to God, "I will trust in you. . . . I will not be afraid." Repeatedly in the psalms we find the determination to trust God—choosing to trust Him despite all appearances. David's declaration in Psalm 23:4, "I will fear no evil," is equivalent to "I will trust in God in the face of evil." In Psalm 16:8 he says, "I have set the LORD always before me. Because he is at my right hand, I will not be shaken." To set the Lord before me is to recognize His presence and His constant help, but this is something we must choose to do.

God is always with us. He has said, "Never will I leave you; never will I forsake you" (Hebrews 13:5). There is no question of His presence with us. But we must *recognize* His presence; we must set Him always before us. We must choose whether or not we will believe His promises of constant protection and care.

Margaret Clarkson, in speaking of how we may arrive at a place of acceptance of adversity in our lives, said, "Always it is initiated by an act of will on our part; we set ourselves to believe in the overruling goodness, providence, and sovereignty of God and refuse to turn aside no matter what may come, no matter how we feel."[1]

For many years in my own pilgrimage of seeking to come to a place of trusting God at all times—I am still far from the end of the journey—I was a prisoner to my feelings. I mistakenly thought I could not trust God unless I felt like trusting Him (which I almost never did in times of adversity). Now I am learning that trusting God is first of all a matter of the will, and is not dependent on my feelings. I choose to trust God and my feelings eventually follow.

Having said that trusting God is first of all a matter of the will, let me qualify that statement to say that, first of all, it is a matter of knowledge. We must *know* that God is sovereign, wise, and loving—in all the ways we have come to see what those terms mean in previous chapters. But having been exposed to the knowledge of the truth, we must then choose whether to believe the truth about God, which He has revealed to us, or whether to follow our feelings. If we are to trust God, we must choose to believe His truth. We must say, "I will trust You though I do not feel like doing so."

Be Willing to Believe

To trust God in times of adversity is admittedly a hard thing to do. I do not mean to suggest in my emphasis on choosing to trust God that the choice is as easy as choosing whether or not I will go to the store, or even choosing whether or not I will do some sacrificial deed. Trusting God is a matter of faith, and faith is the fruit of the Spirit (Galatians 5:22). Only the Holy Spirit can make His Word come alive in our hearts and create faith; but we can choose to look to Him to do that, or we can choose to be ruled by our feelings of anxiety or resentment or grief.

John Newton, author of the hymn "Amazing Grace," watched cancer slowly and painfully kill his wife over a period of many months. In recounting those days, John Newton said:

> I believe it was about two or three months before her death, when I was walking up and down the room, offering disjointed prayers from a heart torn with distress, that a thought suddenly struck me, with unusual force, to this effect—"The promises of God must be true; surely the Lord will help me, *if I am willing to be helped!*" It occurred to me, that we are often led . . . [from an undue regard of our feelings], to indulge that unprofitable grief which both our duty and our peace require us to resist to the utmost of our power. I instantly said aloud, "Lord, I am helpless indeed, in myself, but I hope I am willing, without reserve, that thou shouldest help me."[2]

How was John Newton helped? First he chose to be helped. He realized it was his duty to resist "to the utmost of our power" an inordinate amount of grief and distraction. He realized it was sinful to wallow in self-pity. Then he turned to the Lord, not even asking, but only indicating his *willingness* to be helped. Then he said, "I was not supported by lively sensible consolations, but by being enabled to realize to my mind some great and leading truths of the word of God."[3] The Spirit of God helped him by making needed truths of Scripture alive to him.

He chose to trust God, he turned to God in an attitude of dependence, and he was enabled to realize certain great truths of Scripture. Choice, prayer, and the Word of God were the crucial elements of his being helped to trust God.

The same David who said in Psalm 56:4, "In God I trust; I will not be afraid" said in Psalm 34:4, "I sought the LORD, and he answered me; he delivered me from all my fears." There is no conflict between saying, "I will not be afraid" and asking God to deliver us from our fears. David recognized it was his responsibility to choose to trust God, but also that he was dependent upon the Lord for the ability to do it.

Again, let me emphasize that trusting God does not mean we do not experience pain. It means we believe that God is at work through the occasion of our pain for our ultimate good. It means we work back through the Scriptures regarding His sovereignty, wisdom, and goodness and ask Him to use those Scriptures to bring peace and comfort to our hearts. It means, above all, that we do not sin against God by allowing distrustful and hard thoughts about Him to hold sway in our minds. It will often mean that we may have to say, "God I don't understand, but I trust You."

God Is Trustworthy

The whole idea of trusting God is, of course, based upon the fact that God is absolutely trustworthy. That is why we've looked at His sovereignty, wisdom, and love in previous chapters. We must be firmly grounded in those scriptural truths.

We must also lay hold of some of the great promises of His constant care for us. One such promise we will do well to store up in our hearts is Hebrews 13:5: "Never will I leave you; never will I forsake you." The Puritan preacher Thomas Lye remarked that in this passage the Greek has five negatives and may thus be rendered, "I will not, not leave thee; neither will I not, not forsake thee."[4] Five times God emphasized to us that He will not forsake us. He wants us to firmly grasp the truth that whatever circumstances may indicate, we must believe, on the basis of His promise, that He has not forsaken us or left us to the mercy of those circumstances.

We may sometimes lose the *sense* of God's presence and help but we never lose them. Job, in his distress, could not find God. He said:

> "But if I go to the east, he is not there;
> if I go to the west, I do not find him.
> When he is at work in the north, I do not see him;
> when he turns to the south, I catch no glimpse of him.
> But he knows the way that I take;
> when he has tested me, I will come forth as gold."
> (Job 23:8-10)

Job apparently wavered, as we do, between trust and doubt. Here we see a strong affirmation of trust. He couldn't find God anywhere. God had completely withdrawn from Job the comforting sense of His presence. But Job believed, though he couldn't see Him, that God was watching over him and would bring him through that trial as purified gold.

You and I will sometimes have the same experience as Job—perhaps not in the same kind or intensity of sufferings—but in the seeming inability to find God anywhere. Even the prophet

Isaiah said to God on one occasion, "Truly you are a God who hides himself, O God and Savior of Israel" (Isaiah 45:15). In times of our distress, we must cling to God's bare but inviolate promise, "Never will I leave you; never will I forsake you."

We are invited in the words of Peter to "cast all your anxiety on him because he cares for you" (1 Peter 5:7). God cares for you! Not only will He never leave you—that's the negative side of the promise—but He cares for you. He is not just there with you; He cares for you. His care is constant—not occasional or sporadic. His care is total—even the very hairs of your head are numbered. His care is sovereign—nothing can touch you that He does not allow.

The casting of our anxieties on Him is again a matter of choice. We must by an act of the will in dependence on the Holy Spirit say something such as, "Lord, I choose to cast off this anxiety onto You, but I cannot do this of myself. I will trust You by Your Spirit to enable me, having cast my anxiety on You, not to take it back upon myself."

Trust is not a passive state of mind. It is a vigorous act of the soul by which we choose to lay hold on the promises of God and cling to them despite the adversity that at times seeks to overwhelm us.

Several years ago I encountered a series of related difficulties within a few days. Not major calamities, but of a nature as to cause me great distress. At the outset, the verse Psalm 50:15 came to my mind, "Call upon me in the day of trouble; I will deliver you, and you will honor me." I began to call upon God asking Him to deliver me, but it seemed the more I called, the more the difficulties came.

I began to wonder if God's promises had any real meaning.

Finally one day I said to God, "I will take You at Your Word. I will believe that in Your time and in Your way, You will deliver me." The difficulties did not cease, but the peace of God did quiet my fears and anxieties. And then, in due time, God did deliver me from those troubles, and He did it in such a way that I knew He had done it. God's promises are true. They cannot fail because He cannot lie. But, to realize the peace they are intended to give, we must choose to believe them. We must *cast* our anxieties upon Him.

Pitfalls in Trusting

As difficult as it is to trust God in times of adversity, there are other times when it may be even more difficult to trust Him. These would be times when circumstances are going well, when, to use David's expression, "The boundary lines have fallen . . . in pleasant places" (Psalm 16:6). During times of temporal blessings and prosperity, we are prone to put our trust in those blessings, or even worse, in ourselves as the providers of those blessings.

During times of prosperity and favorable circumstances, we show our trust in God by acknowledging Him as the provider of all those blessings. God caused the nation of Israel to hunger in the desert and then fed them with manna from heaven in order to teach them "that man does not live on bread alone but on every word that comes from the mouth of the LORD" (Deuteronomy 8:3).

So how about us with our cupboards and refrigerators filled with food for tomorrow's meals? We are just as dependent upon God as the Israelites were. God rained down manna for them each day. For us He may provide a regular paycheck and plenty of food at the supermarket ready for us to buy. He provided the Israelites' food through a miracle. He provides our food through a long and complex chain of natural events in which His hand is visible only to the eye of faith. But it is still His provision just as much as was the manna from heaven.

How often are our expressions of thanksgiving at mealtimes hardly more than a perfunctory ritual with little genuine feeling? How often do we stop to acknowledge God's hand of provision and to thank Him for other temporal blessings such as the clothes we wear, the house we live in, the car we drive, the health we enjoy? The extent to which we genuinely thank God for the blessings He provides is an indicator of our trust in Him.

Solomon said, "When times are good, be happy; but when times are bad, consider: God has made the one as well as the other" (Ecclesiastes 7:14). God makes the good times as well as the bad times. In adversity we tend to doubt God's fatherly care, but in prosperity we tend to forget it. If we are to trust God, we must acknowledge our dependence upon Him at all times, good times as well as bad times.

Another pitfall we need to watch for is the tendency to trust in God's instruments of provision rather than in God Himself. In the usual course of events in our lives, God provides for our needs through human means rather than directly. He provides for our financial needs through our vocations and gives us medical personnel to treat us when we are ill. But these human instruments are ultimately under the controlling hand of God. They succeed or prosper only to the extent that God prospers them. We must be careful to look beyond the means and human instrumentalities to the God who uses them.

In Proverbs 18:10-11, there is a very interesting and instructive contrast drawn between the righteous and the rich. The passage says:

The name of the LORD is a strong tower;
the righteous run to it and are safe.
The wealth of the rich is their fortified city;
they imagine it an unscalable wall.

The contrast is not between the righteous and the rich in an absolute sense, as there are many people who are both righteous and wealthy. Rather we should see the contrast drawn between the two primary objects of man's trust: God and money. Those who trust in the Lord *are* safe; while those who trust in their wealth only *imagine* they are safe.

There is a much wider principle for us in this passage. All of us tend to have our fortified cities. It may be an advanced college degree with its ticket to a guaranteed position, or our insurance policies, or our financial nest egg for retirement years. For our nation, it is our military preparedness. Anything other than God Himself that we tend to trust in becomes our "fortified city" with its imagined unscalable walls.

This does not mean we are to disregard the usual means of supply God has provided. It means we must not trust in them. The psalmist said, "I do not trust in my bow" (Psalm 44:6), but he did not say, "I have thrown it away." We must look in trust to God to *use* the means He has provided. While my first wife was battling cancer, we sought expert medical diagnosis and treatment. We looked to God that, according to His will, He would give wisdom and guidance to the doctors. Though we respected the medical skill of the physicians, we knew God gave them that skill and that only He could prosper that skill in any given situation.

We should also keep in mind that God is able to work with or without human means. God is not dependent upon means that we can foresee. In fact, it seems from experience that God delights to surprise us by His ways of deliverance to remind us that our trust must be in Him and Him alone.

Still another pitfall to trusting God, which we are prone to fall into, is to turn to God in trust in the greater crisis experiences of life while seeking to work through the minor difficulties ourselves. A disposition to trust in ourselves is part of our sinful nature. It sometimes takes a major crisis, or at least a moderate one, to turn us toward the Lord. A mark of Christian maturity is to continually trust the Lord in the minutiae of daily life. If we learn to trust God in the minor adversities, we will be better prepared to trust Him in the major ones.

Philip Bennett Power, a nineteenth-century Anglican minister, wrote:

> The daily circumstances of life will afford us opportunities enough of glorifying God in Trust, without our waiting for any extraordinary calls upon our faith. Let us remember that the extraordinary circumstances of life are but few; that much of life may slip past without their occurrence; and that if we be not faithful and trusting in that which is little, we are not likely to be so in that which is great. . . . Let our trust be reared in the humble nursery of our own daily experience, with its ever recurring little wants, and trials, and sorrows; and then, when need be, it will come forth, to do such great things as are required of it.[5]

But whether the difficulty is major or minor, we must learn to say with the psalmist, "When I am afraid, I will trust in you."

Discussion Questions

1. What role does each of these play in trusting God?
   will (choice, decision)
   knowledge
   feelings

2. a. What feelings does David express in Psalm 56?
   b. Where do you see the choice to trust, as an act of will, at work in this psalm?

3. Why does God deserve your trust?

4. a. When we're anxious, sometimes there's something we can do, and sometimes there isn't. Make a list of things you're anxious about.
   b. What action do you need to take?
   c. What do you need to leave in the Lord's hands?

5. Are you more able to trust God than when you began this study? If so, what has helped? If not, what do you think is still missing for you?

GIVING THANKS ALWAYS

Give thanks in all circumstances,
for this is God's will for you in Christ Jesus.
1 THESSALONIANS 5:18

Writer Ellen Vaughn lived in dread of the day her mother would die. Born when her mother was forty-three, Vaughn lived much of her life in fear of losing her aging parent. When that "dreaded day" came—after Vaughn had grown up and married—she was surprised that in the midst of her grief there also came something she hadn't counted on: "The day I had dreaded all my life became the doorway to real renewal." Sorrow over her mother's death also "unleashed an absolute flood of gratitude that has rushed like a river over my life. . . . Death makes it clear that each day of life is an opulent gift."[1]

Ellen Vaughn goes on to tell the stories of individuals who endured much greater suffering than hers—such as the story of an American pilot, tortured in Vietnam's infamous "Hanoi Hilton," and that of a Catholic priest, horribly mistreated in war-torn

Beirut by his Hezbollah captors. Vaughn explains that these men survived by gratitude. She then points to the source of their gratitude: the glory of God, such as that seen by the prophets Ezekiel and Isaiah.[2] Vaughn writes:

> [W]hen we gain our reference point for all things from His cosmic grandeur and holiness—rather than from within ourselves—He will bear us up. Looking up to God's enormity can give us a place to rest and the capacity to give thanks, even in unspeakable tragedy.[3]

Our God is glorious, and in this book we've been looking at three features of that glory: His sovereignty, His wisdom, and His goodness. Because of these, we can *trust* Him. And if we are to honor Him in our times of adversity, we *must* trust Him. For there is more at stake than experiencing peace in the midst of difficulties or even deliverance from them. The honor of God should be our chief concern. So, our primary response to the trustworthiness of God should be, "I will trust God." But there are some important responses that help us progress in trusting God.

Thanksgiving

In our chapter text Paul said to "give thanks in all circumstances." We are to be thankful in bad times and good times, for adversities as well as for blessings. *All* circumstances, whether favorable or unfavorable to our desires, are occasions for gratitude.

Thanksgiving is not a natural virtue; it is a fruit of the Spirit, given by Him. On our own, we are not inclined to give thanks.

We may welcome circumstances that satisfy our wishes and complain about those that are not, but it's not natural for us to give thanks. One of the most indicting statements in the Bible about natural man is Paul's charge that "although they knew God, they neither glorified him as God nor gave thanks to him" (Romans 1:21).

Thanksgiving is an admission of dependence. Through it we recognize that in the physical realm, God "gives [us] life and breath and everything else" (Acts 17:25). And in the spiritual realm, it is God who made us alive in Christ Jesus when we were dead in our transgressions and sins. Everything we are and have we owe to His bountiful grace. "For who makes you different from anyone else? What do you have that you did not receive?" (1 Corinthians 4:7).

As God's children, we are to give Him thanks in *all* circumstances, both the good and the bad. In his gospel, Luke tells the story of ten lepers who were healed by Christ (see Luke 17:11-19). All ten cried out to be healed, and all ten actually experienced Christ's healing power, but only *one* came back to Jesus to thank Him. How prone we are to be as the other nine, quick to ask for God's help, but so forgetful to give Him thanks. In fact, our problem is far deeper than mere forgetfulness. We assume a spirit of ingratitude because of our sinful nature. So, we must cultivate a new spirit, the spirit of gratitude, which the Holy Spirit has implanted within us at our salvation.

Now we all can see the logic in the story of the ten lepers: They all should have returned to give Jesus thanks. We may even acknowledge that many times we have been like the nine forgetful men, when we should have been like the one. We have no trouble with the theology of the story, even if we fail in the application. In this sense, we have no problem accepting Paul's directive to give thanks in all circumstances.

The time when we have difficulty accepting Paul's instruction is when our circumstances are bad. Suppose one person is healed from a dreadful disease while another contracts one. Paul's theology is that both, as believers, should give thanks to God.

Again, what's the basis for giving thanks? God's sovereignty, wisdom, and love, as they are brought to bear upon all the unexpected and sudden shifts and turns in our lives. In short, it is the firm belief that God is at work in all things for our good. It is the willingness to accept this truth from God's Word and rely upon it without having to know exactly how He is working for our good.

We can see a very close connection between the promise of Romans 8:28 and the command of 1 Thessalonians 5:18, when we understand that the literal translation of the words *in all circumstances* is "in everything." In the Greek, as in the English language, the words and meanings are very close. We are to give thanks *in everything* because we know that *in all things* God is at work for our good.[4]

Further, we must realize that God is at work in a proactive, not reactive, fashion. That is, God does not just respond to an adversity in our lives to make the best of a bad situation. He knows before He initiates or permits the adversity exactly how He will use it for our good. God knew exactly what He was doing before He allowed Joseph's brothers to sell him into slavery. Joseph recognized this when he said to his brothers, "So then, it was not you who sent me here, but God. . . . you intended to harm me, but God intended it for good" (Genesis 45:8; 50:20).

Worship

Another response to the trustworthiness of God is to worship Him in times of adversity. When the initial disaster struck Job, the Scripture says,

> He fell to the ground in worship and said: "Naked I came from my mother's womb, and naked I will depart. The LORD gave and the LORD has taken away; may the name of the LORD be praised." (Job 1:20-21)

Instead of reacting against God in the time of his calamity, Job worshiped Him. Instead of raising his fist in the face of God, he fell down before Him. Instead of defiance, there was a humble recognition of God's sovereignty—God in His sovereignty had given, and God in His sovereignty had a right to take away.

Worship involves a two-directional view. Looking upward, we see God in all His majesty, power, glory, and sovereignty as well as His mercy, goodness, and grace. Looking at ourselves, we recognize our dependence upon God and our sinfulness before Him. We see God as the sovereign Creator, worthy to be worshiped, served, and obeyed, and we see ourselves as mere creatures, unworthy sinners who have failed to worship, serve, and obey Him as we should.

We are continuous debtors, not only for God's sovereign mercy in saving us, but for every breath we draw, every bite of food we eat. Everything is of His grace. Everything in heaven and earth belongs to Him, and He says to us in the words of the landowner to the workers in his vineyard, "Don't I have the right to do what I want with my own money?" (Matthew 20:15).

Worship from the heart in times of adversity implies an attitude of humble acceptance of God's right to do as He pleases in our lives. It is a frank acknowledgment that whatever we have at any given moment—health, position, wealth, or anything else we may cherish—is a gift from God's sovereign grace, and may be taken away at His pleasure.

But God does not act toward us in bare sovereignty, wielding His power oppressively or tyrannically. God has already acted toward us in love, mercy, and grace, and He continues to act that way toward us as He works to conform us to the likeness of Christ.

As we bow in worship before His almighty power, we can also bow in confidence that He exercises that power for us, not against us. So we should bow in an attitude of humility, accepting His dealings in our lives. But we can also bow in love, knowing that those dealings, however severe and painful they may be, come from a wise and loving heavenly Father.

Humility

The immediate connection of the thoughts in 1 Peter 5:6-7 should be encouraging to us in times of adversity. The two verses say:

> Humble yourselves, therefore, under God's mighty
> hand, that he may lift you up in due time. Cast all
> your anxiety on him because he cares for you.

On the one hand, we are to humble ourselves under God's mighty hand—an expression equivalent to submitting with a spirit of humility to God's sovereign dealings with us. And on the other hand, we are to cast our anxieties on Him knowing that He cares for us. The anxieties, of course, arise out of the adversities that God's mighty hand brings into our lives. We are to accept the adversities but not the anxieties.

Our tendency is just opposite. We seek to escape from or resist the adversities, but all the while cling to the anxieties they produce. The way to cast our anxieties on the Lord is through humbling ourselves under His sovereignty and then trusting Him in His wisdom and love.

Humility should be both a response to adversity and a fruit of it. The apostle Paul was very clear that the primary purpose of his thorn in the flesh was to curb any tendency toward pride. He said, "To keep me from becoming conceited because of these surpassingly great revelations, there was given me a thorn in my flesh, a messenger of Satan, to torment me" (2 Corinthians 12:7). If Paul had a tendency toward pride, surely we do also. Therefore, we can put it down as a principle: Whenever God blesses us in any way that might engender pride in us, He will along with the blessings give us a "thorn in the flesh" to oppose and undermine that pride. We will be made weak in some way through one or more adversities in order that we might recognize that our strength is in Him, not in ourselves.

We can choose how we will respond to such a thorn in the flesh. We can chafe under it, often for months or even years, or we can accept it from God, humbling ourselves under His mighty hand. When we truly humble ourselves before Him, we will in due time experience the sufficiency of His grace, for "God opposes the proud but gives grace to the humble" (James 4:6).

Forgiveness

Adversity often comes to us through the actions of other people. Sometimes those hurtful actions are deliberately directed at us. At other times we may be the victim of another person's irresponsible actions that, though not deliberately aimed at us, nevertheless affect us seriously. How are we to respond to those who are the instruments of our adversity? The answer, of course, is with love and forgiveness.

Our tendency is to blame the other person, to harbor resentment, and to even desire revenge. I have found that two truths help me forgive others. First, I myself am a sinner, forgiven by the grace of God and the shed blood of His Son. I have hurt others, perhaps not so often deliberately but unconsciously through an uncaring spirit or selfish actions.

Ecclesiastes 7:21-22 says, "Do not pay attention to every word people say, or you may hear your servant cursing you—for you know in your heart that many times you yourself have cursed others." While there is a rich direct application in this passage, there is also a broader principle that speaks to the subject of forgiveness. We can see it by restating the idea of the passage as follows: "Do not resent other people who are the instruments of adversity in your life, for you know in your heart that you have sometimes been the instrument of adversity in the lives of others."

God tells us to forgive each other, just as in Christ He forgave us (Ephesians 4:32). If I want God to forgive me when I have hurt others, then I must be willing to forgive those who are instruments of pain in my life.

Second, I seek to look beyond the person who is only the instrument to see God, who has purposed this adversity for me.

"Who can speak and have it happen if the Lord has not decreed it?" (Lamentations 3:37). If God has ordained to allow this trial in my life, it is because He has in His infinite wisdom deemed it to be good for me. Through the adversity, wrought by the other person, God is doing His work in my life. One part of humbling myself under His mighty hand is to resist any tendency of bitterness or resentment in my heart toward the other person. Though his actions may be sinful in themselves, God is using those actions in my life for my good.

Prayer for Deliverance

A spirit of humble acceptance toward God or forgiveness toward others does not mean we should not pray for deliverance from the adversities that come upon us. Scripture teaches just the opposite. A number of the psalms, for example, contain very fervent prayers for deliverance from troubles of various sorts. Most of all, we have the example of the Lord Jesus Himself, who prayed, "My Father, if it is possible, may this cup be taken from me. Yet not as I will, but as you will" (Matthew 26:39).

As long as the ultimate outcome of an adversity is in doubt (for example, in the case of sickness or a spiritually rebellious child), we should continue to pray, asking God to change the situation. But we should pray this in the same spirit as Jesus did—not as we will but as God wills. We certainly must never demand of God that He will change the situation.

We should also pray for deliverance from the attacks of Satan. As we have already seen, Satan's attacks, like the injuries of other people (such as terrorism or sexual abuse) or the calamitous events of nature (such as earthquakes or hurricanes), are under the sovereign control of God. Satan cannot attack us without the permission of God or go beyond the limits that God has set (see Job 1:12; 2:6; Luke 22:31). We do not know why, in a specific instance, God allows Satan to attack us. But sometimes the reason is that we may engage in spiritual warfare—that we may "resist the devil" (James 4:7).

We should pray for deliverance, and we should learn to resist the attacks of Satan in the power of Jesus Christ. But we should always pray in an attitude of humble acceptance of that which is God's will. Sometimes God's will is deliverance from the adversity; sometimes it is the provision of grace to accept the adversity. Trusting God for the grace to accept adversity is as much an act of faith as is trusting Him for deliverance from it.

Seeking God's Glory

Above all else, our response to adversity should be to seek God's glory. We see this attitude illustrated in the life of the apostle Paul during his imprisonment in Rome. Not only was he imprisoned, but there were men—supposedly fellow ministers of the gospel—who were actually trying to add to his troubles by their preaching (Philippians 1:14-17).

What was Paul's response? He said, "But what does it matter? The important thing is that in every way, whether from false motives or true, Christ is preached. And because of this I rejoice" (Philippians 1:18). Essentially Paul said, "It really doesn't matter what happens to me or how I am affected by all of this, the important thing is what happens to the gospel."

Most of us have probably not progressed that far in our Christian maturity. We have not attained to the degree of selfless spirit that Paul had. It still does matter what happens to us. But this should be our goal, and if we watch for opportunities to grow in that direction, we will see them.

Perhaps you have a certain position of responsibility in your church or a ministry organization. What if someone comes along who is more gifted than you, and you are asked (perhaps not very graciously) to step aside in favor of that person? How will you respond? Here is your opportunity to grow in the direction of being concerned only for God's glory. If you will respond to God in this and humble yourself under His mighty hand, you will experience His grace enabling you to be concerned primarily—if not entirely—with His glory. You will have grown more into the likeness of Jesus, who laid aside His glory to die for you.

Above all, you must see the hand of God in this event, knowing that He, who does all things well, intends this only for your good.

One last quotation from the pen of Alexander Carson will help us to not only see this typical event in its proper perspective, but also to draw together all the gracious truths we have learned in these studies:

> Nothing can be more consoling to the man [or woman]
> of God, than the conviction that the Lord who made
> the world governs the world; and that every event,
> great and small, prosperous and adverse, is under the
> absolute disposal of him who doth all things well, and
> who regulates all things for the good of his people. . . .
> The Christian will be confident and courageous in
> duty, in proportion as he views God in his Providence
> as ruling in the midst of his enemies; and acting for the

good of his people, as well as for his own glory, even in the persecution of the Gospel.[5]

Can You Trust God?

We have seen that God is in control and that He is trustworthy. He is absolutely sovereign over every event in the universe, and He exercises that sovereignty in an infinitely wise and loving way for our good.

So, let me ask: Can *you* trust God? Is your total relationship with God one on which you can build a bulwark of trust against the attacks of adversity? You cannot trust God in isolation from all other areas of your life. To grow in your ability to trust God in times of adversity, you must first lay a solid foundation of a daily personal relationship with Him. Only as you know Him intimately and seek to obey Him completely will you be able to establish a trust relationship with God.

And then, to that foundation of a life lived in communion with God, we must add what we have learned about God in this book—about His sovereignty, wisdom, and love. We must lay hold of these great truths in the little trials as well as the major calamities of life. As we do this in dependence upon the enabling power of His Holy Spirit, we will be able more and more to say, "God is in control, and I can trust Him."

Discussion Questions

1. Why should we thank God in all circumstances?
2. Does 1 Thessalonians 5:18 mean we should thank God that a child died or a divorce occurred? Explain.

3. What is worship?

4. Why should we worship God especially in times of adversity?

5. Why is humility an important response to adversity?

6. How does understanding God's sovereignty help us forgive?

7. Which of these responses to adversity do you most need to concentrate on cultivating at this stage of your life? Why did you choose that one?

> thanksgiving
> worship
> humility
> forgiveness
> prayer for deliverance
> seeking God's glory

NOTES

Chapter 1

1. Allan Laing, "Wave that beggared my belief," (Glasgow: *The Herald*, January 4, 2005), 14.
2. Beliefnet.com, from a continuing poll during 2005.

Chapter 2

1. Harold S. Kushner, *When Bad Things Happen to Good People* (New York: Avon Books, 1983), 42-43.
2. Kushner, 43.
3. From the article by J. I. Packer on "Providence" appearing in *The New Bible Dictionary* (London: The InterVarsity Fellowship, 1962), 1050-1051.
4. Quoted by John Blanchard, *Gathered Gold* (Welwyn, Hertfordshire, England: Evangelical Press, 1984), 332.
5. Andrew Murray, *Every Day with Andrew Murray*, as quoted by *Christianity Today*, March 6, 1987, 41.
6. Gregory A. Boyd, *Is God to Blame?* (Downers Grove, IL: InterVarsity, 2003), 125.
7. Margaret Clarkson, *Grace Grows Best in Winter* (Grand Rapids: Eerdmans, 1984), 40-41.
8. Wym Kayzer, *A Glorious Accident* (New York: W.H. Freeman and Company, 1997).
9. Kushner, 46-48.

10. Kushner, 59.

11. Alexander Carson, *Confidence in God in Times of Danger* (Swengel, Pa.: Reiner Publications, 1975), 25.

12. Philip E. Hughes, *Hope for a Despairing World* (Grand Rapids, Mich.: Baker, 1977), 40-41.

13. Kushner, 43.

14. Margaret Clarkson, *Destined for Glory* (Grand Rapids, Mich.: Eerdmans, 1983), 6.

15. G. C. Berkouwer, *The Providence of God* (Grand Rapids, Mich.: Eerdmans, 1983), 23.

Chapter 3

1. Charles Bridges, *An Exposition of the Book of Proverbs* (Evansville, Ind.: The Sovereign Grace Book Club, 1959), 364.

2. Basil Manly, Sr., *Southern Baptist Sermons on Sovereignty and Responsibility* (Harrisonburg, Va.: Sprinkle Publications, 1984), 15-16. Manley was both a pastor and educator. He was president of the University of Alabama from 1838 to 1855 and was also one of the founding fathers of the Southern Baptist Convention.

3. Richard Fuller, *Southern Baptist Sermons on Sovereignty and Responsibility*, 112.

4. G. C. Berkouwer, *The Providence of God* (Grand Rapids, Mich.: Eerdmans, 1983), 140-141.

5. Alexander Carson, *Confidence in God in Times of Danger* (Swengel, Pa.: Reiner Publications, 1975), 55.

Chapter 4

1. Mike Nichols, "How's the Weather?" *Christian Herald* (July-August 1984), 33.
2. G. C. Berkouwer, *The Providence of God* (Grand Rapids, Mich.: Eerdmans, 1983), 85.
3. Alexander Carson, *The History of Providence* (Grand Rapids, Mich.: Baker, n.d.), v.
4. Alexander Carson, *Confidence in God in Times of Danger* (Swengel, Pa.: Reiner Publications, 1975), 4-5.
5. Edward J. Young, *The Book of Isaiah, vol. 3* (Grand Rapids, Mich.: Eerdmans, 1984), 201.
6. Quoted from a printed copy of a message, "The Sovereignty of God," preached by Dr. Donald G. Barnhouse, n.d., 2.

Chapter 5

1. *Puritan Sermons 1659–1689*, a collection of sermons by seventy-five Puritan preachers, originally published at irregular intervals between 1660 and 1691, in London (Wheaton, Ill.: Richard Owen Roberts, Publisher, 1981), Vol. 1: 374.
2. John Flavel, *The Works of John Flavel* (Edinburgh: The Banner of Truth Trust, 1982), Vol. IV: 336–497.
3. *Puritan Sermons 1659–1689*, Vol. 1:374.
4. Alexander Carson, *Confidence in God in Times of Danger* (Swengel, Pa.: Reiner Publications, 1975), 55.

Chapter 6

1. Brian H. Edwards, *Not by Chance* (Hertfordshire, England: Evangelical Press, 1982), 14.
2. J. L. Dagg, *Manual of Theology* (Harrisonburg, Va.: Gano Books, 1982 edition of original 1857 edition published by The Southern Baptist Publication Society), 86–87.
3. John Piper, *Desiring God* (Portland, Ore.: Multnomah, 1986), 23.
4. Quoted from a very old, undated and unsigned article in the author's file from a British publication, *A Witness and a Testimony*.
5. Margaret Clarkson, *Destined for Glory* (Grand Rapids, Mich.: Eerdmans, 1983), 19.
6. Edward J. Young, *The Book of Isaiah, vol. 3* (Grand Rapids, Mich.: Eerdmans, 1984), 383.
7. C. H. Spurgeon, *God's Providence* (Choteau, Mont.: Gospel Mission, n.d.) 19.
8. G. C. Berkouwer, *The Providence of God* (Grand Rapids: Eerdmans, 1983), 88.
9. John Flavel, *The Works of John Flavel* (Edinburgh: The Banner of Truth Trust, 1982),Vol. III: 361.

Chapter 7

1. Theologians, in speaking of the goodness of God, usually distinguish between His goodness of excellence (as in, he's a good engineer) and His goodness of benevolence (as in,

he's good to his children). In this chapter I use the goodness of God as His benevolence to His people and use it
interchangeably with His love.

Chapter 8

1. Quoted by C. H. Spurgeon, *The Treasury of David* (Grand
   Rapids, Mich.: Baker, 1984), Vol. IV: 306.
2. One method that helps us to remember God's lessons
   through adversity is to keep a journal—a record of these
   lessons—and review them periodically.

Chapter 9

1. Margaret Clarkson, *Grace Grows Best in Winter* (Grand
   Rapids, Mich.: Eerdmans, 1984), 21.
2. John Newton, *The Works of John Newton*, Vol. 5: 621-622.
3. John Newton, *The Works of John Newton*, Vol. 5: 623-624.
4. Puritan Sermons 1659–1689, Vol. 1: 378.
5. Philip Bennett Power, *The "I Wills" of The Psalms* (Edinburgh: The Banner of Truth Trust, 1985, first published
   1858), 63.

Chapter 10

1. Ellen Vaughn, *Radical Gratitude* (Grand Rapids, Mich.:
   Zondervan, 2005), 22.
2. See especially Ezekiel chapter 1 and Isaiah chapter 6.

3. Vaughn, 144-145.

4. There is a discussion among commentators as to whether the wording of the *King James Version* "all things work together for good" in which the *all things* is the subject of the verb work or whether as in the *New International Version* translation in which the subject is God—"in all things God works"—is the preferred wording. Whichever wording we prefer, the result is the same. If all things work together for our good it is because God has *caused* them to do so. In fact, the *New American Standard Bible* translates as follows: "God causes all things to work together for good."

AUTHOR

Jerry Bridges was a well-known Christian writer and conference speaker. His best-known book, *The Pursuit of Holiness*, has sold well over a million copies. A prolific author, he sold over 3.5 million copies of his various books, with several titles translated and published in a variety of foreign languages. He joined the staff of The Navigators in 1955, serving for sixty years as a staff member in various capacities before transitioning to an associate staff position and serving within the collegiate ministry. Jerry passed away in the spring of 2016, leaving behind his wife, Jane; two married children; and seven grandchildren.

READ FROM BEGINNING TO END.

The Word was first, the Word present to God, God present to the Word.
—John 1:1

978-1-61747-949-6
$19.99

978-1-61291-487-9
$64.99

978-1-57683-916-4
$34.99

THE**MESSAGE** is a reading Bible translated from the original Greek and Hebrew Scriptures by Eugene Peterson. With THE**MESSAGE**'s distinctive single-column design, you'll enjoy reading the Bible as much as your favorite book!